A GUIDE TO

FORT STEELE

HISTORIC PARK

Province of
British Columbia
Ministry of
Recreation and
Conservation
Parks Branch

Copyright © 1978 by the Ministry of Recreation and Conservation

Illustrations by Dianne Bersea

First edition: 1978

Canadian Cataloguing in Publication Data

British Columbia.   Parks Branch.
    A guide to Fort Steele Historic Park.

    ISBN 0-7718-8049-9

    1. Fort Steele Historic Park, B.C.   I. Title.

  FC3815.F6B7   917.11'45   C78-016005-3
  F1089.F6B7

Printed in Canada

Contents

Map of Fort Steele Historic Park

Welcome to Fort Steele

In 1961, the historic town of Fort Steele was created a Provincial Historic Park. Since that time, more than fifty displays have been assembled to recreate a typical East Kootenay town at the turn of the century, showing how people of the area lived and worked.

The park contains both restored and reconstructed buildings from the original town, as well as newly constructed buildings which would have been typical to the area during the period between 1890 and 1905. Some of the structures, such as the Roosville Customs House and the Perry Creek Water-Wheel, have been moved in from other parts of the region. Equipping and furnishing the buildings in the park is an ongoing project, and the cooperation and assistance of interested members of the public are welcomed.

Fort Steele Historic Park also functions as a regional museum, collecting, conserving, and interpreting the East Kootenay heritage for the education and enjoyment of present and future generations. While the main emphasis is on the period 1890 - 1905, you will also find exhibits portraying the Kootenay Gold Rush of the 1860s and the period of Indian unrest which brought Superintendent Samuel Steele and "D" Division of the North West Mounted Police to the district in 1887-8. Where space permits, consideration is also given to the archaeology and ethnology of the pre-Gold Rush period and to the history of the East Kootenay region following the decline of Fort Steele.

The park takes the approach to history that the whole town serves as a "living museum." As its tumbled-down buildings are being brought to life again, Fort Steele Historic Park invites you to discover and appreciate the past which has helped to shape the present.

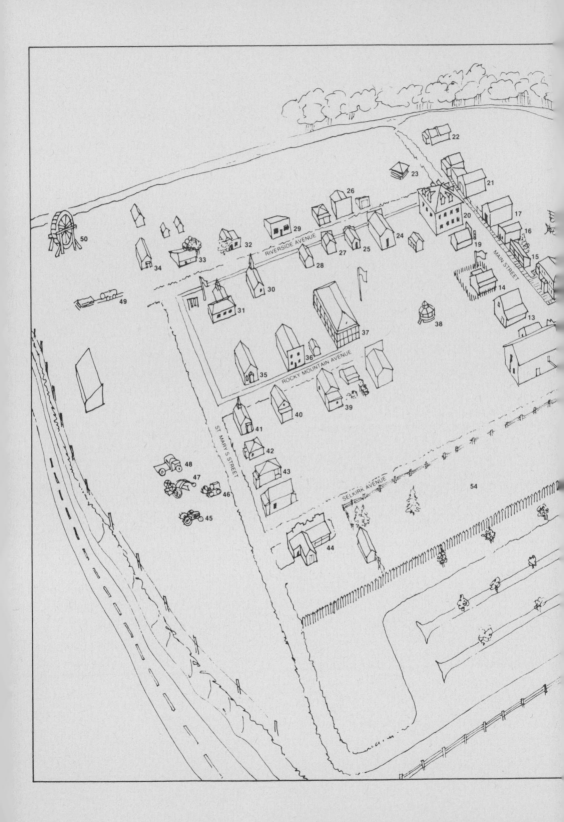

1. The North West Mounted Police Workshop and the National Historic Monument

By 1887, the encroachment of white settlers into East Kootenay had caused considerable unrest among the Upper Kootenay Indians. In the face of a threatened uprising, the Dominion Government sent Superintendent Samuel Steele and a detachment of 75 North West Mounted Police from "D" Division to the Kootenay, in order to investigate and resolve the conflicts.

On July 31, 1887, the Division arrived at the small community of Galbraith's Ferry. The following day, Steele detailed parties to begin construction of several log houses which were to serve as headquarters for the police. Although the "Kootenay" post, as it was officially called, was occupied by the force for only a little over one year, it nevertheless had the distinction of being the first North West Mounted Police post west of the Rockies.

The buildings were originally located on the other side of the present highway. The only structure that survives is the Officers' Quarters (4) which was moved into the interpretation area of the park in 1964 for the purposes of displaying and interpreting the compound. The other buildings (1-3 and 5-8) are reconstructions from the originals, based largely on examination of historic photographs, information recorded in Steele's Annual Reports, and investigations of the Officers' Quarters for structural details.

All the buildings were built of yellow pine logs with saddle-notched corners, floored with common lumber and roofed with shakes. The work of erecting these quarters was not easy, as about 1400 logs of various sizes had to be cut and hauled a considerable distance. The spaces left between the logs were chinked with a mixture of clay and grass, which provided effective windproofing.

This building was used as the general workshop for the post and housed the blacksmith's, carpenters', and saddler's shops. "D" Division included six artisans who were kept busy on a number of different tasks. Furniture had to be made for the barracks, wagons repaired, saddles and harnesses cared for, and general maintenance attended to. They were also responsible for making nails, hinges, latches, and any rudimentary hardware that was needed.

The plaque on the large stone marker at the entrance to the police compound was erected by the Historic Sites and Monuments Board of Canada in 1928 to commemorate the achievements of Steele and the North West Mounted Police.

2. Sergeants' Mess, Kitchen and Quarters

The North West Mounted Police had been formed in 1873, primarily to establish law and order in Canada's old North West Territories (which included most of the area now occupied by the provinces of Manitoba, Saskatchewan, and Alberta). Although the rebellion of the Métis under Louis Riel in Manitoba in 1870 had been dispersed, the Métis were still unhappy with the transfer of their lands to the Dominion of Canada, and whiskey pedlars were creating havoc among the Indians to the west.

As the Government of Canada did not feel that a large military force was required to combat the lawlessness and disorder, it created a civilian force organized along military lines. Although at first the force was not intended to number more than 300 men, it included a commissioner, superintendents, inspectors, sub-inspectors, a paymaster, surgeons, a veterinary surgeon, sergeants, corporals, and constables. "D" Division's ranks ranged from officers to non-commissioned officers to other ranks. The Division's non-commissioned officers included a sergeant major, three staff sergeants and two sergeants. Following military precedent, the officers, non-commissioned officers and the "men" resided in separate quarters.

This building, occupied by the non-commissioned officers, was divided into three parts. On the right were the sleeping quarters, which would have been shared by the sergeants. The centre room was the mess and was used as a common living area for eating meals and passing off-duty hours. On the left was the kitchen where the Division's meals were prepared, but they would have been served in the individual barrack buildings.

Beds were made from sawn planks with only straw mattresses for comfort. Such Spartan usage was not a conscious attempt to instill hardiness in the men. Instead, it was an attempt to provide rudimentary beds in a district at a time when it was extremely difficult to import more comfortable ones. Steele wrote in his Annual Report for 1888, "I beg to suggest that iron bed-cots be provided for use in the barracks, the present wooden trestles being only makeshift and cause great inconvenience and loss of space during the day."

3. Orderly Room and Jail

The orderly room served as the headquarters for the Orderly Officer, the non-commissioned officers, and the men on duty, whose responsibilities included mounting the guard, receiving visitors, looking after prisoners, waking the cooks, and other day-to-day chores around the camp.

According to Steele, there was very little crime in East Kootenay following the arrival of the force. His first task was the controversial case of two Indians accused of murdering and robbing two miners in 1884. As the trial took place while the police were still living in tents, Steele was compelled to use the old jail at Wild Horse Camp, a few miles up Wild Horse Creek from the post.

The task of holding the trial and settling the Indian question was a special mission undertaken by the force upon a request made by the Provincial Government to the Dominion. British Columbia had its own constabulary and only drew upon the services of the North West Mounted Police when situations arose which the provincial police could not handle by themselves. The first time the force had entered the province was during the construction of the Canadian Pacific Railway (1883 to 1885) when it policed the "railway belt." After the completion of the railroad, the force was withdrawn without establishing a single post. The Kootenay incident brought them back on their second mission.

Among the men of "D" Division, discipline and conduct were generally good, although there were twelve desertions from the time the police reached Golden to the time they left East Kootenay. Steele noted that desertion usually occurred in the first year of service and that it was generally committed by "those accustomed to a roving life or who have lived in large cities, where sources of amusement are numerous, or those who have got into debt and are disheartened thereby." Far more reliable, he felt, were "young Canadians or Englishmen of good education and farmers' sons and respectable mechanics from the Canadian Provinces." Steele had the foresight to suggest that recreation facilities, gymnasiums, libraries, and army-style canteens might improve morale and reduce the number of desertions.

13

4. Officers' Quarters

Except for a little more living space, the Officers' Quarters differed very little from the non-commissioned officers' and men's quarters. The interior was finished with the same kind of sawn planking on the floors, walls, and ceiling. While most of the furniture was manufactured by the Division's carpenter, Steele's writing desk and chair were imported from the east.

The officers of "D" Division included Superintendent Steele, Inspectors Z.T. Wood and C.F.A. Huot, and Assistant Surgeon F.H. Powell. They were responsible for providing leadership and attending to the administration of the post. Acting in the capacity of Steele's lieutenants, Inspector Wood was responsible for the field operations, supervising the outposts and patrols, shipping supplies from Golden, and other related duties, while Inspector Huot was mainly in charge of the camp activities, with duties such as supervising drills and target practice, assisting Steele on long marches, and carrying out minor administrative details. Assistant Surgeon Powell was responsible for the post's health and general welfare.

Steele's posting to East Kootenay was only one episode in a lengthy career with the force. His outstanding record helped to create the image of the legendary "Mountie" of sterling character, who figures so largely in popular myth and literature, and is seen so often in comic books and motion pictures. A firm believer in order and discipline without being overly strict, Steele won the respect of the men under his command and the public alike by his just and humane dealings. During the course of his career, he participated in the most colourful campaigns in the annals of the force and served at some of its best known posts. He commanded Mounted Police detachments which patrolled the railway belt during the construction of the Canadian Pacific Railway in 1882-3 and 1884-5, and which first brought him to British Columbia; he was active during the North West Rebellion of 1885, where he was present at Frenchman's Butte and led the pursuit of Big Bear and the Wood Crees; and from 1898-9 he was in charge of the detachments in the Yukon during the Klondike Gold Rush. After the turn of the century, Steele left the force and commanded Lord Strathcona's Horse during the Boer War. Returning to Canada, he soon rose to the rank of Major General and served as Inspector General of Western Canada for the Canadian Permanent Force. His last posting was in England during the Great War, when he was in charge of the Canadian Units in England and where he commanded Shorncliff Military Academy. For his various services to Canada and the Empire, Steele was invested with membership of the Victorian Order, made a Companion of the Order of Bath, and created a Knight Commander of the Order of St. Michael and St. George.

5. Hospital

Disease and sickness, ever a danger to men on a campaign, soon surfaced and emphasized the need for a hospital at the post. Shortly after the Division's arrival in East Kootenay, an outbreak of typhoid (or "mountain fever," as it was often called) took the lives of Constables Lazenby, Mason, Fisher, and Mitchell.

On September 24, 1887, Assistant Surgeon Powell contracted the disease and was unable to attend to the sick. Fortunately, his father, Dr. Israel Powell, the Indian Commissioner for British Columbia, was in the district with a commission inspecting the Indian reserves and was able to lend his services. He remained until October 10, when Assistant Surgeon Paré arrived from Calgary. Paré stayed with the Division until the younger Powell recovered and was again able to perform his duties.

During this outbreak, a venturesome young Englishman named William Adolphe Baillie-Grohman was in the vicinity and left a somewhat grisly account in his book *Sport and Life*. Baillie-Grohman was operating a sawmill on the site of present-day Canal Flats when two of Steele's men, who were stricken with the disease, arrived from Golden. Word was sent quickly to Steele that they were too ill to ride, and a day later a sergeant arrived with a wagon to take them back to the post. Baillie-Grohman relates that "it was raining heavily at the time, and as the driver had forgotten to bring the canvas wagon cover, the doctor's instructions to the sergeant to bring with him as much inch lumber as he could find room for were acted upon, by lashing a sort of roof over the wagon-bed in which the sick men lay. Death is habitually taken in a lighter vein by western men than it is among more civilised surroundings, where accidents are rare, but nevertheless the sergeant's reply, when I asked him for what purpose those inch boards were required at the fort, must have seemed of grim significance to the invalids lying there in plain hearing. 'Oh,' said the sergeant, 'the doc told me that if the men were looking bad, I should bring enough lumber along to bury them with, for they have more dead men than lumber at the fort, and whipsawing ain't healthy (in) this weather.'" To this account the narrator added: "the sergeant wasn't out very far, one of the men, we heard, was dead when the post was reached, and the other one 'used up the balance of lumber' a day or two later, as the driver laconically wrote to one of my men."

6. Barracks

The barracks provided the sleeping, eating and recreational accommodation for the other ranks of the force, which included the corporals and the constables. It simply contained two large rooms separated by a central passage. The rooms were not partitioned and both sides were used as quarters. Although it was large enough to contain all the men, there was little personal privacy.

The entire force was rarely in the camp at one time. In addition to numerous patrols, which were conducted throughout the entire district, a number of parties were stationed at various temporary outposts to ensure that law and order were maintained and that further conflicts between the Indians and white men did not occur. Transporting stores from the CPR station at Golden also occupied much of the force's time. Four men with teams and part of the pack train were kept busy hauling oats and other supplies from Canal Flats, just south of Columbia Lake. A non-commissioned officer and three constables were in charge at Geary's Landing; one constable was stationed at Canal Flats and a non-commissioned officer and two constables were in charge of the horses kept at Arthur Fenwick's Ranch.

When the men were in camp, their time was occupied with drills and riding, sword, manual, and firing exercises. Steele wrote that "during the winter months the men were thoroughly instructed in the duties of a constable, as laid down in the *Constable's Manual*, Inspectors Wood and Huot each taking their sub-division every other night until the entire book had been thoroughly gone through."

7. Quartermaster's Store

This was where the Division's supplies were kept. Items ranged from extra clothing and kit to material for the repair of arms, ammunition, stationery, tools, and camp equipment, and to such miscellaneous items as mosquito netting, flags, ropes, glue, axle grease, and even gold lace for the uniforms.

In the 1880s, East Kootenay was an isolated part of British Columbia. Except for beef, potatoes, and fuel, which could be obtained locally, nearly all the supplies had to be shipped from the old North West Territories and kept in the Quartermaster's store. Consequently, supplies had to be ordered well in advance of when they were needed. Furthermore, it was often exceedingly difficult to get enough of what was required. The clothing supply, for instance, was largely depleted by early 1888, but the Force was not able to recoup its losses until it reached Fort McLeod in August of that year.

Added to the great distance which the supplies had to be sent, transportation facilities from the railway station at Golden to the post were anything but adequate. A combination of river steamers, small boats, wagons, and pack trains had to be used, and the river steamers were particularly unreliable. During high water they could reach the south end of Upper Columbia Lake, but when the seasonal water reached its lowest ebb, they could only go up the Columbia River as far as Spillimacheen, just forty miles south of Golden. As an additional burden, the steamers themselves were extremely untrustworthy. Hastily constructed with shoddy materials, the earliest ones were designed with an eye to profit, with little regard for the safety of the passengers and cargo alike. On her first trip transporting supplies for Steele, the *Duchess* was overloaded and not properly trimmed, and consequently capsized, losing most of her cargo. The *Clive* was then engaged, but as it now had the monopoly of the river, the owner, a Mr. J.C. Hayes, charged exorbitant rates. One delay followed another as Hayes stopped for every prospective passenger with the hope of increasing his already inflated profits. Upon the boat's arrival at Upper Steam Boat Landing, Steele had to send Inspector Wood back to Golden on the *Clive*, because, as he pointed out, "it was evident that unless an officer was there to look after Hayes, there would be little chance of getting any work done by the steamer *Clive*."

8. Stables

The stables were constructed to accommodate seventy-five horses which the force had brought from the North West Territories. Only a few horses, however, were kept in the stables at one time. The majority were constantly used on patrols or kept out on the range at Fenwick's Ranch, ten miles south of the post. After the arrival of the Force at Galbraith's Ferry, Steele purchased twenty-four ponies and three mules to freight supplies, and they also had to be kept in the stables when they were at the post.

Due to the ruggedness of the terrain and the district's few and poor roads, horseback riding was the only practical manner of conducting patrols and transporting supplies. The horses were used on patrols through the Moyie Pass between the Purcell and Selkirk Mountains which led to Sand Point, Idaho; along the Walla Walla Trail, almost due south; and north along the Wild Horse-Golden Trail. Shorter patrols were conducted to the old camp at Wild Horse, Joseph's Prairie (on the site of present day Cranbrook), the St. Eugene Mission, Chief Isadore's camp, and other nearby locations. In the year 1888, Steele estimated that his men had covered an incredible distance of 45,037 miles on horseback.

On the whole, the horses were a success and Steele was pleased with their hard work and good performance. During the summer months, however, they quickly became fatigued. With the hot weather, steep and dusty trails, poor pastures and swarms of mosquitoes to endure, many did not fully recover until the cooler autumn weather. The poor pastures particularly presented a problem, as they produced an inferior quality hay. Horses had to be kept on the ranges well on into the winter and oats had to be imported from the east as the district could not produce enough to feed the entire herd. The problem was compounded by a local crop failure in 1887, which further reduced the feed. Even importing oats did not greatly help, because large quantities were spoiled en route from Golden.

9. Water Tower

The rapid growth of Fort Steele which began in 1896 made it necessary for the town to have an adequate and dependable supply of fresh water. Until then, the inhabitants had been forced to drink the muddy waters of the Kootenay River, after it was hauled up to the town by teams and sold at the exorbitant rate of twenty-five cents a barrel.

In May 1897, preliminary steps were taken for the incorporation of a company to install a water supply system for domestic purposes and fire protection. A committee was formed to investigate feasible proposals, but little was heard from them again. As the weeks dragged on, the weather got warmer, the Kootenay River got muddier, and the Fort Steele *Prospector* became more and more impatient. One June 26, 1897, the newspaper declared, "Water water everywhere, but the inhabitants of Fort Steele must drink beer or go thirsty," and on July 3, it exclaimed that "if Fort Steele residents are to be supplied with water, at any time during the next decade, it is high time something was being done to attain that end."

On July 10, 1897, the Fort Steele Water Works Co. Ltd. was finally formed. The town was canvassed to buy stock. A number of creeks were investigated as possible sources, but eventually a large well was selected, fed by a number of springs and located below the bluff at the south end of Riverside Avenue. A pumping station was installed, and on the bench directly above, a water tower was constructed with a 17,000-gallon holding tank. Water was pumped into the tank and circulated through the mains by gravity. In case of fire, the water was pumped directly from the power house. By February 1898, the system was put into operation, complete with fire hydrants, and shortly thereafter a fire brigade was formed.

This tower, constructed in 1967, is a replica of the original one, which still stands at the south end of town. The reconstruction is presently used as a lookout and is open for the public to view the panorama which surrounds the park.

25

10. Express and Stage Line Office

During the 1890s, Fort Steele was still an isolated town, 160 miles from the Canadian Pacific Railway depot at Golden and 110 miles from the Great Northern station at Jennings, Montana. The lifeline that connected Fort Steele with the railways consisted of stagecoaches, freight wagons, and river steamers. While the steamers could only operate when river conditions permitted, the stagecoaches and freight wagons kept the transportation routes open year-round.

Regular stage service between Fort Steele and Golden began in 1892 with the completion of the wagon road connecting the two towns. A major carrier on this route was the Upper Columbia Navigation and Tramway Company, which also operated sternwheelers on the navigable sections of the intervening lakes and rivers between Fort Steele and Golden. Another major overland transportation route linked Fort Steele with Tobacco Plains and Kalispell. In 1897, two stage lines were operated along this road, one managed by D.W. Stryker out of Kalispell, the other by D.W. Woodbury out of Fort Steele. The Stryker company stage left Kalispell on Saturday at 8:00 a.m., passed through Tobacco Plains on Sunday at 12:00 a.m., and arrived at Fort Steele on Monday evening. During the nineties, several smaller stagecoach companies also provided transportation to nearby locations such as Wardner and Moyie.

One of the transportation outfits operating from Fort Steele in the 1890s was the Mail Stage Line running to Golden and back. On January 23, 1897, one of their wagons was robbed, the first crime of its kind in the area in many years. The incident, however, bore little resemblance to the stage robberies of literature and motion pictures. Alexander M. Leitch, a small-time criminal, was the culprit. Sometime in the evening of January 23, Leitch stole a well-known horse in Fort Steele and rode to Wasa, thirteen miles to the north, where he knew the mail wagon would be stopped overnight. He lifted the mail bag from the unguarded wagon and then returned to Fort Steele where he released the horse. Because the animal was easily tracked and identified as belonging to Charles Levett, a local hotel owner, it was only a matter of hours before Leitch was arrested by Fort Steele's constable, Harry Barnes. The inept robber was caught in his cabin, the $1100 take from the crime beside him and the town's mail making a cheery blaze in his fireplace.

27

11. Wildhorse Theatre

The avid desire for theatrical entertainment is one of the most familiar features of the development of the western frontier. It had been a characteristic aspect of life since the rapid expansion of the American West during the 1850s and 60s, when such towns as San Francisco and Virginia City were particularly well known for their theatres. In their various forms, dramatic performances were highly acclaimed in the mining communities and quickly became a popular form of diversion from the rigours of the miners' lives. With the mining boom which occurred throughout East and West Kootenay during the 1890s, the well known frontier theatre made its appearance in southeastern British Columbia.

Before many of these towns had theatres (or "opera houses" as they were often generously called), hotels, saloons, and community or church halls were used as theatres. In Fort Steele, the first performances were held in the Dalgardno Hall (located in the Dalgardno Hotel, later renamed the Windsor — see 20) or in the schoolhouse (31 and 41). Dramatic tastes varied from amateur performances which included songs, recitations, instrumental solos, comedy sketches, and magic acts, to boxing matches and even an exhibition of "Mrs. Jarley's Wax Figures."

In 1897, Coventry's Opera House, later renamed the Fort Steele Opera House, opened its doors (36). It was a combined theatre and dance hall on the ground floor, with rooms for secret societies and a social club on the second. During the same year, the Fort Steele Elite Minstrels, a local amateur group, was formed and gave the occasional performance. Their repertoire was typically diverse, ranging from choruses, vocal trios, solos, and sayings "wise and otherwise," to farces, buck dancing and "the old plantation hoedown."

From 1898 on, these spirited amateurs were complemented by the occasional appearance of travelling professional troupes which included Fort Steele in their circuits. The level of sophistication varied. The town could expect anything from the team of Birt and Viola, which produced light vaudeville skits, to the Metropolitan Opera Company, which presented Balfe's "The Bohemian Girl." Farces, vaudeville acts, light operas, melodramas, and minstrel shows, however, were the most common type of production.

The Wildhorse Theatre is not a restoration of a theatre which existed in Fort Steele. Instead, it was constructed by the Parks Branch and opened in 1972, to present this aspect of Kootenay life.

12. Government Building

Constructed in 1897, the Government Building contained the offices of the Gold Commissioner, Government Agent, Mining Recorder, Judge of the Court of Revision and Appeals, and District Registrar, as well as minor administrative offices, a court room, and a jail. As impressive as this sounds, in actual fact, with the small population of East Kootenay, one official often held several titles. For instance, James F. Armstrong was the Government Agent, Stipendiary Magistrate, and Gold Commissioner, while Charles M. Edwards was both the Mining Recorder and District Registrar. This practice had continued since the days of the gold rush when the Gold Commissioner was often the sole embodiment of the colonial administration.

John C. Haynes, who arrived at Wild Horse Creek in July 1864, was the first representative of the colonial government to be posted to East Kootenay. Making good use of the wide powers granted to his position as Gold Commissioner, he quickly established order on the creek and affirmed the legitimacy of British rule throughout the area. Despite its remoteness, its proximity to the United States border and its large number of American prospectors, the camp on Wild Horse Creek was effectively administered by the colonial government centred at New Westminster, over five hundred miles to the west. Haynes and his successors were greatly respected by the prospectors and the orderly camp formed a striking contrast to the often violent and chaotic mining towns of Montana and Idaho.

With the greatly decreased activity during the years following the gold rush, there was little need for many government services. However, during the boom years of the nineties the presence of government offices was looked upon by the citizens of Fort Steele as one of the symbols that made their town the centre of the East Kootenay. Imagine their surprise when early in 1897 their MPP, the powerful Col. James Baker, whom they had extolled at the previous election and who was both the Provincial Secretary and Minister of Mines, announced that he would construct the government building at the fledgling town of Cranbrook, which had been part of his own estate. This overt attempt by Baker to end Fort Steele's role as the administrative centre of the district, combined with his apparent complicity in the routing of the B.C. Southern Railway (now known as the Crowsnest Line of the CPR) through his "instant town," infuriated the townspeople. Scathing editorials appeared in the *Prospector* (29), and Baker forfeited the confidence and trust of Fort Steele's citizens. Although the attacks on Baker's character continued, he quickly reversed his former decision and had this building constructed in Fort Steele during the autumn of 1897. The offices were not to remain in this building for long, however. In 1905 they were moved to Cranbrook.

31

13. Livery Stable

Before the railway came to East Kootenay, and certainly before the automobile, the only feasible mode of travel was on horseback or in some form of horse-drawn carriage. Consequently, the livery stable, wagon shed (15), harness shop (16), and blacksmith's shop (17) were essential services, the equivalent of today's service station, parkade, automotive supply dealer, and auto-body repair shop.

During its heyday, Fort Steele had a number of livery stables. Coaches and freight wagons were constantly arriving and their teams had to be fed and looked after before they could make their return journey. The stables sold horses and hired them out for riding, packing and teaming, complete with all the necessary rigs. Many also included boarding facilities for horses whose owners had nowhere to keep them. One of the businesses, Gilpin and Lindsay, even sold bicycles and grass mowers.

This barn was part of Alfred Doyle's livery stables. Like many men who came to Fort Steele during its boom years, Doyle sought to establish a profitable business by providing a greatly needed service to the thriving and prosperous community. Around 1900, he formed a partnership with another livery-man named George Geary, but in 1907 he went into business for himself, moving his operation to the present location. As well as this barn, he had adjacent corrals, a bunkhouse for his staff, and a small, modest house across from the barn for himself.

With the advent of the automobile, this building, like many other livery stables, was converted into a service station. Doyle, however, proved to be a more successful livery-man than auto mechanic. Shortly before 1920, he brought a "Detroiter" car to Fort Steele, but suffered no end of problems with it. Fortunately, the automobile had not yet totally superseded the buckboard and carriage, and he was able to return to them for the remainder of his days.

33

14. Post Office

From the earliest days of the Kootenay Gold Rush through the 1980s, the remoteness of the Fort Steele area posed many problems in the delivery of mail. Infrequent, irregular and mismanaged, it was a source of constant irritation to East Kootenay residents. Despite an area population in excess of 4000, Fort Steele did not have weekly mail service until well into 1897.

The first post office in East Kootenay was established in 1866 at Fisherville on Wild Horse Creek, but for many years no attempt was made to maintain a regular mail service. Government correspondence from Victoria was carried to the area by special couriers contracted at $150 per trip. These men were not pony express riders trying to get the mail to its destination in the fastest time possible, but simply trustworthy individuals who were willing to make the long and often arduous journey to East Kootenay. Most residents of the Wild Horse Creek area engaged a private express outfit and sent their mail, at considerable cost, through Walla Walla.

Soon after the completion of the Canadian Pacific Railway in 1885, East Kootenay received a nominal mail service, fortnightly from May to October and monthly for the remainder of the year. Mail was sent by train to Golden, where it was transferred either to a mail wagon or river steamer. The latter took the mail upstream only as far as Windermere, where it was placed in a wagon for the remainder of the journey. During winter, the trip from Golden to Fort Steele could be particularly difficult. In one recorded instance, deep snow and intense cold so restricted the progress of the mail carrier that he covered only twenty-seven miles in five days.

In time, the frequency of the mail service to Fort Steele improved, but most inhabitants agreed that the quality of the service did not. The shoddy performance of the post office was a favourite topic of conversation and an oft-used subject of editorials in the *Prospector*. One settler, F.P. Norbury, wrote of the problem in 1889 in letters to his family in England. "I am off tomorrow morning to Golden, having been delayed here a week for the mail which is disgracefully managed or rather not managed at all. The letters being left indiscriminately at each P.O. along the road. Most of Phillipp's mail went to Cranbrook and a letter we wanted particularly about the machinery hasn't turned up yet. I may perhaps find it at Golden." Needless to say, the letter never was found.

15. Wagon Shed

Wagon sheds were usually attached to livery stables. This one was used by Carlin and Durick (21) and also provided storage for feed, hay and various equipment.

Today it contains a selection of horse-drawn rigs from a dray (four wheels and a deck) to a democrat and logging sleighs, all of which were frequently used. Less often seen in East Kootenay was the classic Concord stagecoach, a feature of the frontier invariably included in Hollywood westerns. The Concord, a limousine of stage travel, had a hefty price tag — well over $1500 when delivered to the Pacific Coast. Stage lines operating in East Kootenay used a number of other types of stagecoach besides the Concord, among them the Troy, Celerity, Mud Wagon and Jerky. Less expensive than the Concord, these other varieties were reasonably dependable and did lengthy service on the western frontier.

The hose reel displayed was used for fire fighting. Most of the buildings constructed in Fort Steele were wooden and a fire could easily have destroyed the town in just a few short hours. Consequently, after the town's water supply system was installed in 1897 (9), a relatively effective fire brigade was formed. Hoses, nozzles, hooks, ladders, axes and a hose cart were either ordered or constructed. It was none too soon, because on September 1, 1898, the International Hotel and three smaller buildings were burnt to the ground before the firefighters could extinguish the blaze and stop it from spreading any further.

16. Harness Shop

This small shop sold harnesses, saddles and other items necessary for equipping horses and horse teams. The operator would have been a skilled harness maker with a good working knowledge of all aspects of leather craft. For example, William Doul, an early harness maker in the town, later turned his attention exclusively to shoe-making and repair.

A number of leather-working tools are displayed in this shop, including an early leather sewing machine. Many of the goods sold here, however, would have been made in the larger urban factories. The owner would have ordered the goods required, much the same way retailers order their supplies today. Even so, he still would have been responsible for making specialty items, modifying stock goods upon request, and repairing broken and worn-out pieces.

17. Blacksmith's Shop

Nearly every small town had at least one blacksmith shop. As common as electricians and plumbers are today, blacksmiths were equally as important during the last century and the earlier part of this one, carrying out a number of jobs, shaping and forging metal for many different requirements.

Horseshoeing was one of the well-known tasks. With the vast number of horses needed for land transportation, horseshoeing constantly kept the blacksmiths busy. Even today, the park's herd of Clydesdales have to be shod regularly, although the job is now done in the North West Mounted Police stables (8).

Wheelwrighting was another common chore required of the blacksmith. A metal rim was fitted onto a wooden wagon wheel, first by pre-heating the metal so it would expand to a size greater than the circumference of the wheel, and then by cooling it down with water once it was on the wheel so it would contract and fit snugly to the framework. Occasionally forged nails were fashioned, although by the 1890s they had been largely replaced by less expensive cut-wire nails, which could be purchased in the town's hardware stores. Hooks, hinges, and brackets were among the other items which would have been made by the blacksmith.

There were a number of blacksmiths in Fort Steele, and their advertisements in the *Prospector* give some indication of each one's expertise. For example, J.J. Quinlivan advertised, "General Blacksmith, Wheelwright and Horse-shoeing a specialty," while P.J. Cruickshank declared, "General Blacksmith, Horse-Shoeing and Jobbing. Mining work a specialty."

Closely allied to the blacksmith was the tinsmith. In 1897, T.C. Armstrong opened a tin shop in Fort Steele and advertised himself in the *Prospector* as a "Manufacturer of Tinware, Galvanized Iron, Sheet-Iron, Stove Pipes and Copperware." His jobs included "Buildings heated and ventilated, plumbing, pipefitting and all kinds of sanitary work. Air Tight Hot Blast Stoves. Hydraulic and Air Pipes for Mines. Special Attention paid to job work." His own shop was a testimonial for his work because it displayed a tin roof with galvanized iron siding.

18. Wolf Creek Cabin

The crudely constructed Wolf Creek Cabin is typical of many primitive shelters built by the pioneers on the western frontier. Unlike the more permanent log house, the log cabin was erected to provide immediate shelter from the elements. Once the pioneer had sufficiently settled the new land, he either built a more substantial log house, or if there was a sawmill nearby, a frame house. As a consequence, such cabins were strictly functional with little in the way of architectural embellishment.

The cabin is simply constructed with five roughly dressed logs along its length; these are crudely notched with single lap joints at the corners. A single door and window are little more than openings in the wall. The roof is made of small poplar logs, four to six inches in diameter, laid lengthwise, topped by a layer of slough grass, covered with approximately four inches of dirt and finally finished with split shakes. Although the layer of dirt was inclined to sprinkle the occupants with dust in the dry weather and drip mud in the rain, it did provide a readily available form of insulation to keep them warm in the winter and cool in the summer. A very inventive yet rudimentary technique is used in constructing the fireplace. Instead of erecting a stone chimney, the logs at the south end of the building are extended outwards, forming a triangular-shaped protrusion. The walls are then lined with a non-combustible material, consisting of clay, earth, and fireplace rocks.

Exactly when and for whom this cabin was built is unknown. It could date as early as the Gold Rush period and is, in all likelihood, similar in many respects to those cabins which were built along the banks of Wild Horse Creek and at the sites of other local rushes. It was moved to Fort Steele Historic Park in 1969 from the Wolf Creek Ranch, located some twenty miles north of Fort Steele.

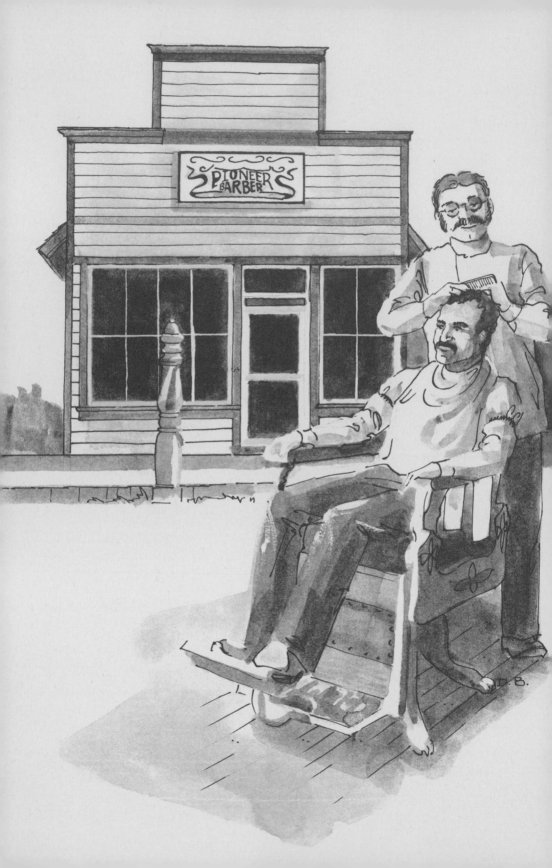

19. Barber Shop

In many of British Columbia's mining towns, one of the first businesses to appear after the hotels and ever-present bars was the barber shop. By 1898, Fort Steele could boast of a number of barbers, of which the most prominent was James Highwarden. A hardworking man, proud of his reputation, he advertised himself as a "tonsorial artist."

Like Wellington Moses in Barkerville and many other barbers on the frontier, James Highwarden was a black man. Whether Highwarden and his family suffered from racial prejudice in a town where anti-oriental sentiment was common is unknown. However, if they did, his business does not appear to have been affected. With his son, Highwarden operated the prosperous barber shop, while his wife looked after a "High Class Bath House" and worked as a dressmaker. The industrious barber also acted as school janitor for a time. The entire family was musically talented and performed in many of Fort Steele's variety shows and concerts. Highwarden was a member of Fort Steele's small but enthusiastic brass band, which was directed by another barber, Albert J. Grez. According to the *Prospector,* Highwarden sold his barber shop to one C.E. Adams in August 1898. He remained in the area after the decline of Fort Steele, and the *Cranbrook Herald* of January 14, 1909, reported his rather bizarre death in the bathroom of his house. "It is supposed that Mr. Highwarden was fixing the pipes connected with the bath which had become frozen, and fell into the bath stunning himself. Whatever the cause, his lifeless body was found frozen."

Highwarden's barber shop, like the drug store in town (24), was something of a social magnet, a meeting place where the men of Fort Steele discussed news items of the day and the latest mining prospects while having a morning shave or haircut. Of interest are some of the features of this turn-of-the-century shop, particularly the numerous shaving mugs, the open or cut-throat razors, the hot water bowl, and the ornate corner sink.

45

20. Windsor Hotel

Built by Robert Mather in the winter of 1893-4, the Windsor Hotel was the best known and one of the largest of the seven hotels operating in Fort Steele during the latter part of the decade. Mather originally called his hotel the Dalgardno House after his wife's maiden name. The building was known by that name until June, 1899. Including a forty-by-sixty-foot annex, which has since been demolished, the hotel boasted twenty-seven furnished rooms, a dining room, a bar, a card room, and a hall.

The Windsor, in addition to its function as a hotel, was Fort Steele's social centre for several years. Numerous dances, entertainments, sports matches and meetings were held in the hall of the hotel. Among the most memorable were the Victoria Diamond Jubilee Ball held on June 22, 1897, as the climax of the day's festivities honouring the aged monarch, and the St. Andrew's Day Celebration, which occurred on November 31, 1897. The latter event, attended by over 150 people, was a dinner and ball, enthusiastically described by the newspaper as "the finest celebration of its kind that has yet taken place in Fort Steele." A banquet of monumental proportions was prepared by Mather and his employees. This feast consisted of two soups, two fish dishes, eight cuts of meat, two types of poultry, three salads, four vegetables, a pudding, three varieties of pie, numerous cakes and biscuits, nuts, raisins, apples, tea and coffee. Equally impressive must have been the liquid refreshments, for the printed menu constantly exhorts the guest to "Tak' a Dram" or "A Wee Drappie."

The Windsor and other hotels in town such as the Venosta, the International, and the Oriental, were usually advertised as "first-class" establishments, which offered "elegance" and "comfort" to tired travellers. While not nearly as elaborate as the pretentious luxury hotels of the period, the Windsor was a considerable improvement over much of the accommodation available in the towns of the Canadian and American frontier. J.A. Lees and W.J. Clutterbuck, two English tourists who visited East Kootenay in 1887, described the sort of hotel most travellers on the frontier were obliged to patronize: ". . . its cheerlessness can hardly be imagined. There is only one public room, which is generally full of roughs, in the spaces between the spittoons. It has a stove in the middle, and smells unpleasantly if windproof; but if, as more usually happens, its walls are largely composed of cracks held apart by logs, the draughts whistle through the apartment with an intensity unknown to good stay-at-home people. Even if you are lucky enough to get within reach of the stove, the only chance of keeping your circulation unfrozen is to warm one side at a time, while the other one rapidly drops to zero."

21. Carlin and Durick General Store

This general merchandise business was only one of several such enterprises in Fort Steele, all of which did an excellent trade in the 1890s. Due to the shortcomings of the transportation system, it was impossible for Carlin and Durick to rely on obtaining goods in sufficient quantities to meet the demands of the rapidly expanding population. As a result, the arrival of a shipment of merchandise at the store was considered a newsworthy event and duly reported in the *Prospector*.

William Carlin and James Durick were both born in Quebec in 1864, and had worked in the East Kootenay for a number of years prior to the formation of their partnership in 1895. Durick, in fact, was only one in a succession of business partners of Carlin, who, over the years, was also extensively involved in logging, ranching, and mining.

An establishment such as Carlin and Durick was the frontier equivalent of the modern department store, its shelves filled with a wide variety of merchandise such as clothing, shoes, mining supplies, and general hardware, food, firearms and ammunition, medicines, tobacco, and jewellery. Beyond that there was also the need to cater to the boom-town demand for imported delicacies and cheap trinkets.

By mid-1898, the town newspaper was claiming with considerable justification that Carlin and Durick was "one of the most prominent and successful business enterprises in the interior of British Columbia." The store had just undergone an expansion when suddenly, on May 7, 1898, the citizens of Fort Steele were shocked to learn of the death by pneumonia of James Durick. Following the demise of his associate, William Carlin devoted less time to the store and more to his other business ventures, but nevertheless retained a part ownership of the firm until his own death in 1932.

The building itself is an interesting conglomeration of different parts which have been successively added on to an original section over a number of years. The oldest part of the structure is probably the front half of the section which was used as the dry goods store. It is a log building and the construction details are clearly evident on the west wall. Such additive structures were common in frontier communities, where buildings were continually enlarged to accommodate growing functions. The "1864" on the building does not indicate the year of its construction, but rather the year in which an earlier store was first established on the site.

22. Galbraith's Ferry Office

Galbraith's Ferry Office is one of the older buildings in Fort Steele. It was constructed by John Galbraith, who came to East Kootenay in 1864 in the vanguard of the prospectors heading for Wild Horse Creek.

At that time all the major trails led into the district from the west side of the Kootenay River. As Wild Horse Creek flows in from the east side, a ford was established just south of the confluence of the Kootenay River and Wild Horse Creek, but it soon proved to be unsatisfactory. Galbraith and a few associates realized the need for a more suitable crossing, so they hastily established a ferry service to freight supplies into the district from Walla Walla.

In 1865, Galbraith received an official lease to operate the ferry and paid a rental of $500 a year. In 1867, this was lowered to $200 a year when traffic had substantially decreased. During the peak years of the rush, users had to pay $10 for each loaded pack animal and $5 for each man. By 1870, the fare had fallen to $1 for animals and 50 cents per man.

In 1870, John was joined by his brother, Robert L.T. Galbraith. Robert assumed most of the responsibility for the business many years before John's death in 1887, and was extremely active in the commercial and public life of East Kootenay until his own death in 1924. As well as looking after the ferry, store, and pack trains, Robert operated a stock farm on Joseph's Prairie (the site of present day Cranbrook), obtained the charter and served as chairman and director for the Kootenay Central Railway, acted as the Indian agent for the district from 1894 until 1921, and was elected to the Provincial Parliament three times. He continued to operate the ferry out of this office until 1888, when a bridge was constructed across the Kootenay River.

Simply known as Galbraith's Ferry, the small community which grew up around the Galbraith's operations was a well-known landmark in the Kootenays during the decades between the gold rush and the boom years of the nineties. Its location on the crossroads of travel and communication in East Kootenay ensured its geographical importance as the country became populated. The community's name was changed to Fort Steele in 1888, to honour Sam Steele and the North West Mounted Police.

23. Roosville Customs House

This building originally served as the Customs House at the small community of Roosville located near the International Boundary in the area of the Kootenay Valley known as Tobacco Plains. Constructed about 1898, it was used until 1916, when it was replaced by a larger building. In 1965 the building was moved to Fort Steele as an example of a modest customs office which was used in East Kootenay around the turn of the century.

The Tobacco Plains area of the Kootenay Valley has long been the access route between Montana and B.C. It was well known to early fur traders, and to Wild Horse Creek gold seekers of the 1860s who travelled the Kalispell Trail. The first Customs office was established at Tobacco Plains in 1896 and soon moved to Crow's Nest Landing to cope with the paddlewheelers plying between Jennings and Fort Steele. Later the offices were moved to Phillipps, Gateway, and Roosville as the mode of travel changed to railway and then to highway.

24. Pioneer Drug Hall

The drug store was an important feature in any town at the turn of the century. As well as dispensing drugs and medicines and selling a wide variety of goods, it was often a meeting place where locals could exchange news and gossip.

In Fort Steele this business was operated by A.W. Bleasdell, who arrived in the town in 1896 after working in Ontario, Manitoba, and the old North West Territories. Of his store he claimed "Nothing 'Cheap' here, but your Money's worth every time."

With its shelves full of chemicals, herbs, patent medicines and "miracle cures" of the period, the Pioneer Drug Store presents quite a different appearance from most modern pharmacies. In the 1890s, the druggist rolled most pills by hand. These medicines often contained massive amounts of morphine, opium and bromides and were usually prepared in front of interested customers, whose chief concern was that the resulting mixture be palatable. Beyond the prescription drugs, there was a wide variety of patent medicines, brightly labelled, endorsed by the famous and the unknown, and offering speedy and effective relief from numerous ailments. Alcohol was a common ingredient in many of these products. Botanical medicines and herbs were very popular during the 1890s. The roots, leaves, flowers or fruit of medicinal plants were used in a great many decoctions, tinctures, salves, and infusions.

In frontier towns, the drug store was usually a retail outlet for many products that we now associate with hardware stores, sporting goods stores, confectioneries, supermarkets, and photographic supply stores. Like Carlin and Durick (21), it was almost a miniature department store. Bleasdell, advertising in the *Prospector,* summed up his operation and others like it. "Some things we have — a full stock of B. Lawrence's English Spectacles and Eye Glasses. The best spectacles in the world. Banjo strings, Razors, Razor Strops, Toilet soaps, Castile soap, Perfumes, Tooth Brushes, Hair Brushes, Nail and Scrub Brushes, Toilet Paper, Toilet preparations, Mirrors, Playing Cards, Stationery, Mouth Organs, Patent Medicines and Drugs of all kinds. Celluloid and hard Rubber Trusses (those goods fitted on the premises), Abdominal Supporters, Suspenders, Surgical Dressings and appliances. Machine oil, Gum oil, Raw oil. In fact, anything and everything you want."

25. Dr. Watt's Office

This building, constructed in 1897, was the office of Dr. Hugh Watt, one of the pioneer physicians of British Columbia. Prior to his arrival in Fort Steele, he had practiced medicine from 1882 to 1897 in Barkerville, where he was surgeon to the Royal Cariboo Hospital. A well-known and popular figure in Fort Steele, Dr. Watt, like most frontier physicians, had a "practice" which covered hundreds of square miles.

At Fort Steele, Watt was appointed Resident Physician and Coroner for the Electoral District of East Kootenay. While he was a familiar figure in Fort Steele, Watt, because of his duties, spent considerable time away from town. One day he would be called upon to hold an inquest into the violent death of a railway worker on the Crowsnest Pass and the next he would have to dash off to deliver a baby near Canal Flats. With the rapid growth of Fort Steele, sanitation became a major problem and it was feared that unless some action was taken disease would break out. Watt was appointed Health Officer for the Mining District and quickly initiated a campaign to improve the town's sanitary facilities, water system and general cleanliness.

Watt was one of the prime movers behind the plan to construct the much needed Victoria Diamond Jubilee Hospital in Fort Steele. It was built in 1897, and remained in operation until sometime after 1905, by which date the town had fallen on hard times. Nevertheless, Watt continued his practice in Fort Steele until 1912, when he retired. He died two years later in nearby Elko.

In addition to his activities in the field of medicine, Watt was a man of many talents and interests. Over the years, he published and edited a newspaper, taught school, mastered six languages and an Indian dialect, and became a prominent Mason and elder of the Presbyterian Church. While in Fort Steele, Watt also acted as a representative for a group of eastern businessmen making investments in the region. Politically active, he served as a Member of the Provincial Parliament for Cariboo, and was a dominent figure in the Liberal Association of East Kootenay. In the latter capacity, Watt lobbied with determination to bring the railroad to Fort Steele.

26. Kershaw Store

Unlike the general merchants, Henry Kershaw operated a combined coffee bar-confectionery. His lunch counter offered "the finest tea, coffee and cocoa," which would be "freshly made and daintily served," with homemade bread, cakes, pastry and "confectionery of all kinds," while the store sold such assorted items as Havana and Mexican cigars, Christmas and layer cakes, pies, mincemeat, chocolate, candies, nuts, eggs, homemade bread and homemade marmalade, and even Californian wines, cider, and fresh Californian fruit when available.

Kershaw had come to Fort Steele with his family in May 1897. He immediately set out to build a large home in which he rented out a few rooms as a guest house and ran a bath house with hot and cold water. In the following year, he constructed a new premises for his lunch counter-confectionery store on Riverside Avenue. The business was a thriving success and many of the town's inhabitants frequented it to enjoy his light meals or to while away the time. In 1906 Kershaw died and in the same year the business burned to the ground.

Henry Kershaw, Jr. who had inherited the business, immediately relocated a similar operation in this building, formerly occupied by the Bank of Commerce. By 1906, however, most people had left Fort Steele. As there was no longer the need for this kind of venture, the younger Kershaw had to re-open the business as a general store as well. In 1901 he had been appointed postmaster and he continued to run the post office out of his store until 1947, when he retired due to ill health.

Henry and his wife, Clara, had nine children, all of whom were born and grew up in Fort Steele. One of the sons, Gordon, and his wife, Ina, continued to operate the store until 1954, when they sold the business and moved away, bringing to an end 57 years of faithful family service to the community.

27. Dentist Office

This is a typical example of a dentist office from the turn of the century. Fort Steele, despite its booming population in 1897, was never able to attract a resident dentist. However, the town was visited on a number of occasions by "travelling dentists."

At the time Fort Steele was in its heyday, dentistry in the province was still in its infancy, with the first legislation to regulate the profession only having been approved in 1886. The shortage of skilled professionals led to many amateurs in the field, particularly in mining camps. Some of these individuals developed a reasonable proficiency, but the majority were a dubious lot. The camp on Wild Horse Creek in the 1860s probably would have had a number of amateur dentists, but by the 1890s most of the dental problems in Fort Steele were being handled by the travelling professionals. Those who could not wait for the periodic visits by dentists, travelled to other towns to have their teeth cared for. A favourite location was Spokane, as the general opinion held was that the Americans were better dentists and less expensive than their Canadian counterparts.

Considering that wages in the 1890s were $3 to $4 per day, dental fees of the time were comparable to today's. In 1893, the dentists of the province established a fee schedule with set rates for various operations. Consultations cost $2.50 to $5.00, extractions were $1.00 per tooth, dentures were $1.00 per tooth with a 50 per cent rebate on completion of the plate, and fillings cost $2.00 to $3.00 for amalgam or composition and $3.00 to $25.00 for gold. In a remote boom town like Fort Steele, however, it is likely that dentists charged more for their services.

The man whose name appears on the sign on the Building, Dr. J. Grice, was one of the travelling dentists who visited Fort Steele in 1897 and 1898. That there was no shortage of work for these men is apparent from articles in the newspaper which stated that anyone wanting dental work done had to be at the dentist's "office" as soon as possible. The "office" was usually a room in one of the hotels.

28. Telegraph Office

Fort Steele suffered from a lack of communication with the outside world for many years. Most news items and information were received in the mails, or came from people arriving in the town by stagecoach or river steamer. The situation worsened in winter, when it could take two weeks for a news story to reach Fort Steele. A significant step towards ending this isolation came with the establishment of a telegraph service between Fort Steele and Kalispell, Montana, on September 1, 1897. The operator of the line was the Spokane and Fort Steele Telegraph Company, apparently a part of the Western Union network.

The first definite word of a proposed telegraph line from Kalispell appeared in the *Prospector* on June 12, 1897. Telegraph company representatives optimistically estimated the line would be operational within forty days. Not surprisingly, the construction time was almost twice the estimate. On September 3, 1897, the *Prospector* ran an enthusiastic account of the completion of the line to Kalispell. Messages were sent to Lieutenant-Governor Dewdney, to the Press Association of Spokane, to the *Spokane Review,* and to the manager of the Spokane Fair. As often happens on such occasions, one thing spoiled the performance. In the midst of the congratulatory messages the line went down, leaving Fort Steele once again without a communication link.

When the telegraph line was repaired a week later, Fort Steele entered a new era. The *Prospector's* news section expanded to accommodate the bulk of information that clicked over the line from Spokane, mining promoters were able to obtain up-to-date quotations from the stock markets, and businessmen were able to purchase goods and supplies with far greater ease and some confidence.

At the same time that the telegraph line was being constructed, preliminary steps were being taken to provide telephone service to the town. This service, completed on March 30, 1898, was operated by the Canada Western Telegraph and Telephone Company. It connected Fort Steele with Moyie, Wardner, Wasa, St. Eugene Mission, and the North Star and Sullivan mines. A complete communication link from Fort Steele to Golden was not established until 1902, when the Dominion Government ran a combined telegraph and telephone line from Golden to Windermere where it connected with the Fort Steele system. The combined line operated until 1908, when the telegraph service was discontinued.

29. Prospector Newspaper Office

Fort Steele's newspaper, the *Prospector*, first appeared on November 9, 1895. One of the province's most unique newspapers, it was the creation of pioneer journalist A.B. Grace, who, in addition to writing most of the newspaper, also contributed numerous drawings and diagrams to illustrate the articles.

During its first year, the *Prospector* was typewritten and reproduced in mimeograph form. The initial press run was 250 copies, but it increased as the population of Fort Steele grew through 1896 and 1897. In May, 1896, Grace was printing 375 copies of his four-page weekly newspaper in five hours on his primitive Edison mimeograph. By mid-1897, Grace and his recently hired staff were turning out several times that number on the company's newly installed Babcock Perfecting Press. The *Prospector* had subscribers as far away as Britain, and even in its infancy it attracted attention on the other side of the continent. The *Fourth Estate*, a New York magazine, noted in early 1896, "Mr. Grace is a versatile genius, and combines with his editorial and reportorial accomplishments that of an artist of no mean order . . . The entire newspaper, with the exception of sketches and diagrams, is typewritten. The general effect is pleasing and the sheet is more easily read than many papers gotten out in the regular way."

A tireless booster of Fort Steele, the *Prospector* had strong editorial opinions on virtually anything which might influence the town's future. The newspaper was forever calling for better transportation facilities, particularly for speedier action on railroad construction and river improvements. Favourite targets for journalistic vitriol were the inadequate postal service and government attempts to increase taxes on mines. Like many mining town newspapers, the *Prospector* supported measures such as the Alien Exclusion Act which was designed to eliminate Oriental immigration. During the provincial election of 1898, the *Prospector* mercilessly attacked the incumbent for East Kootenay, Colonel James Baker. Citing the abuse of his position as Provincial Secretary and Minister of Mines for personal gain, the newspaper came out strongly in support of the opposition candidate, William Baillie. Strangely enough, Baillie was also an editor of the *Prospector*.

30. Saint Anthony's Catholic Church

Fort Steele's first church services were held in the old schoolhouse which was jointly used by the Catholics, Anglicans, and Presbyterians (41). In June 1897, the Bishop of New Westminster, the Right Reverend Bishop Durien, visited the Kootenays and decided that the thriving town of Fort Steele needed a small Catholic Church of its own. He immediately instructed Father Coccola, O.M.I., who was in charge of the nearby St. Eugene Mission, to begin construction on St. Anthony's Church. It was completed on October 31 of the same year. Father Coccola celebrated the opening with the ceremony of blessing the church, followed by High Mass. Thereafter, regular Sunday service was conducted by Coccola's assistant, Father Walsh.

By the time St. Anthony's was opened, Catholic missionaries had been active for many years in East Kootenay. As early as 1845, the Jesuit priest Father De Smet passed through this area, converting many Indians to Christianity. He was followed by others, but a permanent mission was not established until 1874.

In that year, Father Fouquet, O.M.I., and Brother Burns were sent into the district. They established the St. Eugene Mission on the St. Mary's River six miles above its junction with the Kootenay River at Galbraith's Ferry. A log church and school were erected. As well as providing religious instruction, Fouquet, Burns, and their successors were instrumental in changing the Indians' lifestyle from hunting and gathering to farming and stock raising.

In 1887, Father Fouquet was replaced by Father Coccola. The latter was extremely helpful in reconciling the Indian with the white man during the period of unrest which brought Superintendent Sam Steele and the North West Mounted Police to East Kootenay. Under his supervision, a larger school and the majestic St. Eugene Mission church, which still stands just a few miles outside of present day Cranbrook, were constructed. Coccola also travelled extensively throughout the entire Kootenay district — from the Columbia Lakes to Tobacco Plains and over the Moyie Pass to West Kootenay — ministering to the needs of this large parish.

31. Public School

This building was Fort Steele's second schoolhouse, completed in 1898. The town's first schoolhouse, constructed by R.L.T. Galbraith in 1894, was converted later for use as the Anglican Church (41). Prior to 1894, classes were held in a building which is now part of the Carlin and Durick structure (21).

In the 1890s, Miss Adelaide Bailey was Fort Steele's only schoolteacher. Like most frontier teachers, she had to be able to teach all grades, which was quite an undertaking when the school's attendance rose to over seventy pupils. Eventually she was assisted by a monitor, Mrs. M.B. Clark, who took on some of the teaching duties. By today's standards, Miss Bailey's monthly salary of $70 would seem very meagre, but at the turn of the century it was quite reasonable. At that time, depending on the qualifications, teachers' salaries ran from $25 to $135 per month.

During the school year 1898/99, Fort Steele's school had its greatest attendance of ninety pupils. While the number of courses taught in the school was fairly large, it appears that the only subjects taken by all students were reading, writing, spelling and mental arithmetic. Some of the other subjects taught can be easily guessed — history, geography, and composition. However, certain other subjects deemed worthy of inclusion in the course of study might seem a little unusual to people nowadays, among them needlework, mensuration, and temperance. Interestingly enough, one subject missing from the curriculum at Fort Steele and most other rural schools was science. At Fort Steele a student might learn of the evils of demon rum, but little of elementary chemistry, physics, or biology.

32. Bakery

This building and the others south of it on Riverside Avenue strikingly illustrate the fate of most of Fort Steele's buildings. Deserted by businesses which moved to Cranbrook and other towns or went bankrupt, the wooden structures, never built to last, soon fell victim to fire or the ravages of time and climate.

In Fort Steele, a number of stores offered fresh bakery goods for sale. Although it is difficult to find conclusive evidence, it appears that this building was operated by a "Mrs. Wolf" as a bakery and laundry. The remains of the ovens can still be seen at the rear of the building. At Henry Kershaw's lunch counter (26), fresh bread, cakes and pies baked on the premises were sold. By 1898, Fort Steele also had a "German Bakery and Coffee House" run by Frank Peckstein, who offered his customers "Home made Bread and fresh Coffee at all hours."

71

33. Butcher Shop

"Not much, we must say, has been done by the store-keepers this year in the way of holiday decoration, but there is a very attractive exception at 'Malcolm McInnes' butcher shop. The display there of Christmas beef, mutton and poultry is very fine, and it is decorated in a manner so pretty as to induce the holiday purchaser to buy two turkeys where otherwise he might have bought only one."

In this way the *Prospector* described the holiday preparations of one of the more prominent butchers in Fort Steele. McInnes' shop was located on Riverside Avenue, as were those of the town's other butchers. This location was convenient to the bridge over the Kootenay River and would have minimized the need for driving stock for slaughter through the streets of the town. Both Malcolm McInnes and Robson and Rodgers, Fort Steele's other major butcher, sometimes had a difficult time obtaining sufficient meat and poultry to meet the demands of the town, the mining camps, and the railway construction camps. It appears that the butchers or their agents had to make frequent trips as far afield as what is now Alberta to purchase herds of cattle and sheep for slaughter. In May 1898, Fort Steele's newspaper noted the imminent arrival of a hundred head of sheep from Windermere for McInnes' shop with the happy comment that "for a time at least there will be no scarcity of prime mutton." The great demand for meat meant that local ranchers had no difficulty in disposing to the butchers for high prices all the cattle, pigs, sheep, and poultry they could raise. A few ranchers, eager to make more money, did their own wholesale butchering and sold directly to the mining and railway camps. According to F.P. Norbury, one of the ranchers engaged in this practice, the result was a handsome fifty per cent increase in profits.

34. Taenhauser House

Very little is known about the origin and history of this structure. For a short period it was occupied by a Miss Lillian Taenhauser and the name has remained with the building.

The original Taenhauser family house, which has long since burned down, was located across the street. It was constructed by Joe Taenhauser, Lillian's father, who had moved to Fort Steele from Columbia Falls, Montana, in 1897. Here he opened his "watch hospital" and jewellery shop in one half of the house.

Taenhauser was not the only watch repairman and jeweller in Fort Steele. A little earlier, one David Bettchen had also opened a jewellery shop and watch repair business. Today it might seem hard to imagine that a town like Fort Steele had two such businesses, but one must remember that Fort Steele at the turn of the century was East Kootenay's largest settlement.

35. Presbyterian Church

Following in the footsteps of the Catholics and the Anglicans, Presbyterian missionaries entered East Kootenay in the wake of development that followed the completion of the CPR.

During the summers of 1893 and 1894, Reverend A.D. McKinnon administered an area stretching from Golden to Fort Steele. Through his efforts congregations were organized at Fort Steele, Windermere and Galena.

At Fort Steele he began services in the schoolhouse (31), which were continued until the arrival of Rev. John G. Duncan from the Kamloops Presbytery in January, 1898. Rev. Duncan moved the services to the Opera House (36) and took immediate steps to organize a church building committee. The trustees appointed included such prominent citizens as Henry Kershaw (26), Malcolm McInnes, (33), R.D. Mather (39), and Dr. Hugh Watt (25). A Ladies Aid Society was formed to help raise funds for the construction and through talent schemes, soirées, and socials, including an ice cream social, a substantial amount was contributed. By July, tenders were called for construction of the new church, and on September 4, 1898, Rev. Duncan was able to preach the opening service.

The Methodists followed on the heels of the Presbyterians, and although there never was a Methodist church in Fort Steele, their services were occasionally given in this church by visiting Methodist preachers. Together these two denominations began missionary activities in the construction camps along the right of way for the B.C. Southern Railway. Itinerant preachers spread throughout the district and churches were established in the larger towns such as Fernie and Cranbrook. By the end of the century, they were so well established throughout the Kootenays that an independent Kootenay Presbytery and a Methodist District were created.

77

36. Masonic Hall (North Star Lodge No. 30)

Since the Fraser River Gold Rush of 1858, a large number of secret fraternal societies have flourished in British Columbia. The Freemasons were probably the largest and most widespread group. In numerous towns many of the prominent citizens were Masons and through the Order they acted as an important social force in shaping an orderly society. In Fort Steele, many well-known figures were active Masons and left an indelible mark on the political and cultural life of the province. Perhaps the most well-known was Charles Mair, the famous Canadian poet.

The first Masons came to East Kootenay during the gold rush of the 1860s, but like many of the other prospectors, the majority left the district when the mines declined. With the renewed activity of the 1890s, many Masons again settled in the area surrounding Fort Steele. By the end of the decade their numbers had so increased that many felt the time had come when Fort Steele should have its own lodge. A petition was sent to the Grand Lodge of British Columbia and on February 21, 1899, a dispensation was issued authorizing the formation of North Star Lodge No. 30.

This building was constructed in 1897, as the Fort Steele Opera House (11). The Masons shared the second floor with the Kootenay Club, Fort Steele's equivalent to the fashionable men's clubs that were so popular during the nineteenth century. Other secret fraternal societies, such as the Order of Foresters and the Knights of Labour, also occasionally met in the same rooms as the Masons during the years around the turn of the century.

This was also the one building in the town which could accommodate large dances, "balls," civic gatherings and political rallies. The Reverend John G. Duncan even held the Presbyterian church services here before the denomination's church was completed (35).

The building's prominence in the community, however, was shortlived. In 1900, the Kootenay Club constructed its own clubhouse and the Fort Steele Brass Band erected its own hall, which was more suitably equipped to hold dances and theatrical entertainments. Left largely to the Masons, the order took over the entire second storey, which it occupied until 1944, when the North Star Lodge amalgamated with Cranbrook Lodge No. 34.

37. Museum

The Museum is a recent structure specifically built to house some of the Park's collection and serve as an interpretation centre. It is patterned after one of East Kootenay's best-known hostelries at the turn of the century, the Wasa Hotel, which was located approximately twelve miles north of Fort Steele.

During Fort Steele's boom years, the Wasa Hotel was the scene of many long-remembered parties presided over by Nils Hanson, genial hotel owner and renowned host. An annual event at Wasa was Hanson's Christmas party and dance. Guests came from all along the valley, from the United States boundary to Windermere, to partake of the festivities which began before noon and lasted until three or four o'clock the next morning. Each year, as Hanson surpassed all his previous efforts, guests would declare the event the best ever held.

Wasa was a favourite overnight stop on the road from Fort Steele to Golden. A small settlement with little in the way of commercial development aside from the hotel and a sawmill, Wasa was only one of a number of towns which sprang up in East Kootenay in the 1890s. Others were Tracy, Swansea, Wardner, Elko, Kimberley and Cranbrook. Some of these settlements appeared in the wake of railway and road developments and others because of the mineral discoveries. However, the citizens of Fort Steele considered their town the capital of East Kootenay and viewed these lesser hamlets as points on a wheel, the hub of which was Fort Steele. Any town whose citizens dared to presume that their townsite was to be the future centre of development in East Kootenay could be assured of a scathing journalistic attack in the *Prospector*.

On the main floor of the Museum the exhibits and displays provide the visitor with an introduction to the history of Fort Steele and the East Kootenay region. In the upper gallery, special displays, changed annually, illustrate facets of the history of the area in greater detail. Also included in this building are a resource library, artifact storage area, curatorial offices and a tea room where visitors can obtain refreshments. At the desk on the main floor visitors can purchase a variety of books and pamphlets.

38. Bandstand

Around 1900, bandstands could be found in city parks and squares. They provided an attractive focal point for community recreation and amusements. Although there never was one in Fort Steele, outdoor recreation and entertainment played a large and varied role in the leisure time of the town's residents.

Each summer, picnics and excursions took place in the countryside around Fort Steele and large parties often went to Wasa where they were entertained by Nils Hanson (37). In the winter, sleigh rides and skating on the Kootenay River were popular.

As the town grew, organized sports flourished. A football team was formed in 1897, and matches were held on a large square, similar to this one, just to the east of town. Rugby and baseball quickly followed and soon baseball games were held against Moyie. Shortly afterward, a bowling alley and a handball and tennis court were constructed.

Hunting was always a favourite sport and interest in shooting resulted in the formation of the Fort Steele Rod and Gun Club. Trap shoots were held on a semi-regular basis and money prizes were awarded to the winners.

Nearly every official holiday, whether it was the Queen's Birthday, Dominion Day or the Fourth of July, was celebrated with track and field festivities. The events ranged from the more conventional ones, which included the 100 yard dash, high jump and shot put, to horse races, bicycle races, wrestling matches, and a tug of war between such teams as the married men versus the single, Indians versus whites, and "Canada" vs. the "U.S." The day's activities usually were followed with a dance in the evening, held either at the Dalgardno Hotel (the Windsor, 20), or the Fort Steele Opera House (36), with music provided by Fort Steele's own Brass Band or the Indian Boys Band from the St. Eugene Mission.

This present Bandstand, patterned after the Alexandria Park bandstand at Vancouver's English Bay, was constructed in 1967, to serve as a stage for special events and to provide shelter under which a band, similar to Fort Steele's Brass Band of the 1890s, could play to public audiences.

39. Mather House

The rapid growth of Fort Steele's commercial sector during the mid-1890s was paralleled by a sudden rise in the number of private residences. In 1895, Fort Steele was still a small village with few houses, but by 1898, the *Prospector* could boast of 122 residences for the town. Though few houses remain today, those restored in the park show a wide range in type and size, depending upon the wealth and social status of the owner.

This house, originally the home of Robert Duncan Mather and his family, is typical of a moderate-sized home constructed for a citizen of relatively comfortable means. Its style, however, is quite plain, lacking any of the ornate Victorian embellishments which were so popular for many houses built during this period in the larger urban centres. Its conservative design, reflecting the tastes of an earlier period, is typical of numerous houses built on the frontier. Very often, carpenters and builders in pioneer settlements had to rely on the styles with which they were familiar before coming to such communities. They would continue to build in that vein for many years with little innovation or reference to the current architectural fashions. Those modifications which were made were usually taken from architectural copy-books and builders' or trade journals of the period, but such changes were introduced slowly and cautiously.

Robert Mather was a prominent citizen in Fort Steele, and one of the district's pioneer entrepreneurs. Together with his father, Captain James Mather, he imported a herd of Scottish long-haired cattle from Scotland and started a 1000-acre ranch at Cherry Creek (later renamed Mather Creek) just a few miles north of Galbraith's Ferry (Fort Steele). He went on to operate a pack train service to freight supplies into the area, began one of the first local sawmills, and even, for a short time, operated a store on Wild Horse Creek. In 1882, he married Mary Jane Dalgardno of Port Townsend, Washington. Mrs. Mather had to travel to her old home to give birth to the first four of her seven children, as there were no doctors in East Kootenay at that time. In 1893, the family moved to Fort Steele, where Mather built the Dalgardno Hotel (the Windsor, 20). Shortly afterward, he constructed this house. He continued to operate the hotel and sawmill until his death in 1908.

40. Cohn House

This house is essentially a scaled-down and simplified version of the type of home occupied by the Mather family, displaying a very similar distribution of doors and windows along its facade. The running verandah was a typical feature of most urban and rural houses built during the latter part of the nineteenth century. The small ornamental brackets at the head of the posts holding up the verandah's roof are the only examples on the house of what is referred to as Victorian "gingerbread," which was so lavishly used on many buildings during the 1890s.

Frequently referred to as cottages rather than houses, these small residential structures were extremely common during the last century among the lower middle class families. This one is believed to have been first owned by Lewis Cohn, who was a tailor and "importer of woollens." He probably ran a small and respectable business, but as he did not figure prominently in the community, little has been recorded about his activities.

In 1975, an interpretation program was begun in the Cohn House to introduce school children to a number of aspects of domestic life at the turn of the century. In the kitchen, such activities as making butter, baking bread, and carding wool are carried out. These demonstrations attempt to bring a pioneer home alive by enacting chores which were typical of the period.

41. St. John the Divine Anglican Church

This building was constructed in 1894, and served as Fort Steele's first schoolhouse. It was also used as a public meeting hall and church for all the local denominations. The Anglicans met here nearly every Sunday after the building's construction, using the premises for their services and Sunday School.

As the town did not have its own Anglican minister for many years, the sermons were delivered instead by R.L.T. Galbraith, who had been appointed a licenced Lay Reader by the Anglican Bishop of New Westminster. Galbraith discoursed on such topics as the "Anxiety about the Future," "Whispering Whisperers," "The Authenticity of the Bible," "Shall We Know Each Other There," and similarly related topics.

Early in 1898, the Anglicans formed an established congregation and took the name St. John the Divine. An appeal was made to the societies in England for funds to support a resident clergyman, R.L.T. Galbraith donated four lots on Selkirk Avenue for a church and rectory, and a Ladies Guild was established to raise money for the church.

A new church, however, was never built. After the new schoolhouse was constructed (31), the old schoolhouse officially became St. John the Divine as a gift from Galbraith, who still owned the building. With a growing congregation, the church was enlarged with the addition of a choir and vestry.

Finally, in late August, 1898, the Reverend C.A. Procunier arrived in East Kootenay and took up his residence in Fort Steele as the town's first vicar at St. John the Divine.

42. Anglican Vicarage

The vicarage was built shortly after the arrival of the Reverend C.A. Procunier. The St. John's Ladies Guild took care of the formal arrangements, R.L.T. Galbraith donated two lots for the purpose, a loan was taken out to cover construction costs, and by October, 1898, the vicarage was under construction.

When it was completed in March of the following year, the vicarage made a handsome addition to the residences of the town. An attractive one-storey house with a high hipped roof, it is the best surviving example of a "Victorian" house in Fort Steele, with its ornate, pedimented porch, row of small tooth-like dentils under the eaves, panelling under the windows and decorative crestings along the ridge of the roof. Originally situated on the site of the present highway, it was moved to this location as part of the Fort Steele restoration project.

As well as providing the living accommodation for the minister and his wife, the vicarage was also the scene of many social events. Numerous members of the parish joined the couple for afternoon tea, receptions and parties, and the vicar even formed a reading club for Shakespearean study and literature. In small frontier communities such as Fort Steele, the church, whether Anglican, Catholic, Presbyterian, or any other denomination, provided a strong nucleus for many of the town's social activities.

43. Hanson House

Like the Mather House (39), the Hanson House would have been built for a relatively well-to-do middle class family. Its moderately large size, formal facade with a full length verandah, tall, vertical windows and low, hipped roof, are typical features of the "Victorian Villa" which could be found throughout North America during the last quarter of the nineteenth century.

The original owner has not been recorded, but it is believed that this house was built on speculation by Nils "Guvnor" Hanson, much the same way many houses are presently built in our suburbs. It was probably constructed between the years 1897 and 1900, when Fort Steele's population began its meteoric increase, causing the sharpest demand for housing in the town's history. On June 5, 1897, the *Prospector* reported that "the music of the hammer and saw are heard in Fort Steele from early morn to dark, some 40 buildings are under construction and this number could be trebled if the supply of lumber was equal to demand." By 1899, this demand had not abated, and on July 15, the *Prospector* observed that "for some reason which has yet not been made perfectly clear, there is an unprecedented demand for dwelling houses in Fort Steele. This demand is not confined to the people in the town, but the inquiries come from the outside and from people who wish to come to Fort Steele to live. To a casual observer it would appear that if some capitalists in Fort Steele were to erect a few cottages they would realize good interest on their investment. It seems too bad that people who would like to live in Fort Steele must go elsewhere because there are no houses for them to live in." Obviously, Hanson was one "capitalist" who followed up the opportunity.

An interesting feature of this house is the plank frame or box type of construction used. A layer of rough sawn planks has been nailed together vertically to form the wall, and the exterior has been finished with horizontal siding. This method of construction was commonly used on the western frontier, but it has since been superseded by modern nailed frame construction using two-by-four inch studs. A section of wall in an upstairs bedroom has been left exposed to show the planks of an interior wall.

93

44. Sash and Door Factory

This row of storefronts was constructed in 1969 to serve as a "falsefront" for the park's workshop complex. Although it is not an exact replica of a street front which existed in historic Fort Steele, it serves to illustrate part of what a main commercial street looked like in many nineteenth-century boom towns. It has been given the name Sash and Door Factory to commemorate two common trades which flourished during the period from 1890 to 1905.

When Fort Steele began its boom in 1896, the prices for town lots greatly increased. Merchants could not afford to build on large spacious lots, so the familiar pattern in which shops were constructed closely together in irregular rows soon appeared. Each building had its own distinctive and elaborately designed "false-front." These were imitation wooden copies of the pre-cast concrete and cast iron facades of the large commercial buildings which could be found in the major cities such as Victoria, San Francisco, or Portland. These, in turn, had been modelled after the great merchant palaces, banks and town halls of the Italian Renaissance to conjure up the image of a sound and prosperous business establishment. In a time when advertising had not yet reached its present large-scale proportions, the buildings themselves had to attract business through such symbolism. The "false-front" made the building look more important than it actually was.

During Fort Steele's peak years, sash and door factories, contractors and builders, sawmills, lumber yards, painters and decorators, tin shops, and hardware stores conducted a thriving trade in response to the building demands of the burgeoning community. In the summer season of 1897, the sawmills were operating to peak capacity and still could not meet the demands of the town. The Townsite agents, C. Venosta and later T. McVittie, were kept extremely busy selling lots and buildings. This flurry of excitement only subsided when it finally became evident that Cranbrook, and not Fort Steele, was to be East Kootenay's principal town.

45. Fordson Tractor

A common sight on many farms in Canada during the 1930s, the little Fordson tractor was a forerunner of today's large and powerful agricultural tractors. As East Kootenay was not a developed farming area, the first powered farm machinery did not make its appearance until after 1900. The early tractors were enormous steam-powered contraptions which terrified the horses and oxen they gradually replaced. It was only a short time, however, before large steam tractors became obsolete and were succeeded by more compact and useful gasoline-fueled machines. However, these machines were still quite large, and it was not until after the Great War that smaller multi-purpose farm tractors like the Fordson began to appear. The Fordson used a combination of fuels. After using gasoline as a starting fuel, the operator would switch over to stove oil for the duration of the operation.

46. Caterpillar Thirty

The "Cat 30" was a familiar sight on road construction projects and in logging and mining operations throughout Canada and the United States during the 1930s. Introduced by the Best Company in 1921, this machine was given the Caterpillar name in 1925 when the firm merged with the rival Holt Company to form the Caterpillar Tractor Company.

The continuous belt tractor which was to prove so adaptable and useful was originally designed as a solution to a specific problem. At the turn of the century, steam-powered agricultural tractors ran on enormous hardwood wheels. These machines had considerable difficulty operating in the soft peat soil of Central California. Prior to the introduction of the continuous belt tractor in 1904, the most common way of dealing with the problem had been to attach wheels side by side to disperse the weight of the tractor. In some cases the resulting piece of equipment was over forty feet wide.

Compact, with a thirty horsepower gasoline engine, the "Cat 30" was a far cry from the large teams of horses and men required for road construction barely a quarter of a century prior to its introduction. In the Fort Steele area in the late 1890s, crews were constantly employed building new roads and upgrading existing ones. A network of dirt roads linked Fort Steele with the larger mining camps and nearby towns such as Wardner and Elko. Some routes were built and maintained by the Department of Public Works, but many others were private ventures financed by companies eager to exploit the mineral resources of the region. Almost every year, extensive bridge work also was required, as flood waters invariably damaged the numerous river crossings. The great flood of 1894 destroyed or severely damaged every bridge in the district and a significant expenditure of public and private funds was required for the necessary repairs. An interesting illustration of the depreciated value of a dollar is seen in the recorded cost of construction of a large new bridge over the Kootenay River at Fort Steele just after the flood. The entire project cost $17,062.69.

47. Galion Grader

Prior to the introduction of the powered road grader in the late 1930s, grading equipment used in road construction and maintenance was towed behind a separate power source. In Fort Steele's heyday, large teams of horses were used, but these soon were superseded by compact efficient gasoline tractors such as the Caterpiller Thirty (46). In the case of the Galion Grader and others like it, the grader man stood on the back of the machine and operated the controls, while the towing vehicle driver looked after the steering.

48. Federal Truck

The Federal Truck and other industrial relics are examples of the early automated vehicles used in East Kootenay. As well as representing the end of the era typified by Fort Steele, these vehicles heralded the machines of our modern age.

The Federal was just one of many trucks which began to be commonly used for many aspects of general transport in the 1920s. Besides the "homemade" affairs built in machine shops on special order, some of the more well-known ones included the Fagel, Reo, Godfordson, Day-Elder, Fisher-Hayes, White, Leyland, Thornycroft, Diamond T, and Packard, as well as the Federal. To younger generations, many of these names are unfamiliar, although Hayes and White still make some of the larger transport trucks used on the roads today.

Trucks like the Federal greatly altered the logging industry. The steam train was the first fundamental step toward the use of power machinery (47), but in practice its use was really only feasible in heavily forested areas, due to the relatively high cost of laying track. The logging truck, on the other hand, made it possible for outfits to harvest areas with comparative ease quickly moving on from one tract to the next. On the less densely forested hillsides of the interior, the change to the logging truck, which began in the 1920s, was a great boon to the industry.

Today, trucks like the small Federal have been replaced by the gigantic "rigs" which haul logs for East Kootenay's second largest industry.

49. Compressed Air Locomotive

Of great significance in the history of East Kootenay was the discovery and exploitation of the coal fields of the Crowsnest Pass region. As early as the 1890s, the extent and value of these coal beds were realized, but it was not until after 1900 that large scale mining operations began. Among the equipment used in the mines were compressed air locomotives, which appeared at Elk River Colliery prior to 1910, and were in use until the 1960s.

The compressed air locomotive added a welcome element of safety to the operation of coal mines. Hazards, such as smoke, fire and electrical wires associated with the other methods of transporting coal underground, were avoided by using compressed air as a source of power.

At the Elk River Colliery, the compressed air required by the locomotives was generated with a heavy-duty compressor outside the mine and was stored in air receivers at 700 pounds per square inch. A high-pressure pipeline carried the air underground to a number of charging stations located along the tracks at quarter- to half-mile intervals. The locomotives replenished their supply of compressed air by tapping the pipeline, an operation which required up to a minute to complete.

Although a safe form of mine transportation, the compressed air locomotive had its disadvantages. The compressor, air receivers, and distribution pipeline were costly to maintain and the numerous charging stops were inconvenient and time-consuming. In addition, coal mine tunnels were often filled with fog as a result of the cold exhaust from these locomotives. Consequently the compressed air locomotives were replaced by diesel units in the 1960s.

50. Perry Creek Water-Wheel

To many a symbol of Fort Steele Historic Park, this huge water-wheel was originally located at Perry Creek, twenty-five miles west of Fort Steele. It was moved to its present site in 1965. Although the history of Perry Creek as a goldfield dates back to the 1860s, the water-wheel was a part of a mining project undertaken during the Great Depression.

Perry Creek Gold Mines Limited, which built the wheel, hoped to exploit bedrock gold deposits, which, because of their depth below the surface and a combination of water and quicksand, had eluded earlier miners. Unlike many smaller water-wheels used in the province in the nineteenth century, the Perry Creek wheel did not directly activate a simple mechanical system for pumping water from the mine tunnels. Instead, its primary function was to turn a turbine which produced electricity to power two modern pumps for removing water from the mine.

Completed in 1934, the water-wheel was thirty-two feet in diameter and seven feet wide. It was capable of producing sixty-eight horsepower to drive the two pumps. Water pumped from the mine was discharged into a sluice, where it was used to wash the pay dirt hoisted from 150 feet below.

Initially, the wheel did not operate properly, primarily because certain parts were not sufficiently reinforced to deal with the weight of water in the buckets. With a few alterations, however, the wheel ran successfully and it was reported to be so well balanced that a child could turn it from its still position.

The Perry Creek mine was in operation throughout most of 1935, but severe weather conditions forced a temporary closure during the winter. Shortly after work resumed in 1936, word arrived of the unexpected death of George M. Bell, president of the company and father of Max Bell, the mine's overseer. With the subsequent departure of Max Bell to manage the family's newspaper interests in Calgary, the Perry Creek mine ceased operation and was never re-opened.

107

51. Railway Station

This building is the station for Fort Steele Historic Park's railway, which began operation in 1968. Both the station and the trains recall an era when an ever-growing railroad network gave Canada and the United States their first effective land transportation system.

The turn of the century was the golden age of the railroads. Automobiles were little more than curiosities and the road network across the continent was still a web of dirt tracks. Trains were fast, efficient, and in some cases very luxurious. Many railroads claimed to offer first-class accommodation equal to that of the best trans-Atlantic steamers. Passenger cars were filled with sumptuous carpeting, curtains and plush furniture, and the dining car offered an extensive menu designed to please the most discriminating of travellers.

It was also a time when railroads literally made or ruined towns and the construction of the British Columbia Southern, or the Crow's Nest Line as it was also called, was the incident around which Fort Steele flourished and fell. The town's rapid growth was spurred in part by the conviction that Fort Steele would inevitably become the railway's divisional headquarters and a major commercial metropolis. Its decline can be directly attributed to the fact that the railroad, and hence "progress," passed it by in 1897 in favour of the hamlet, Cranbrook.

Many Fort Steele residents continued the fight to bring a line into the town. It was a long and frustrating campaign for Fort Steele's die-hard supporters. Finally, in October 1912, the tracks of the Kootenay Central Railway reached Fort Steele. When this line was completed to Golden in December 1914, Fort Steele had a direct rail link with both the Canadian Pacific Railway main line and the British Columbia Southern. However, it proved too late to revive the dying town.

52. The "Dunrobin"

It would be difficult to imagine two more widely different locomotives than those at Fort Steele. The little "Dunrobin" was originally an aristocratic plaything, specially built to pull the private train of Scotland's Duke of Sutherland, a turn-of-the-century railway enthusiast.

The "Dunrobin" was built in Glasgow in 1894 for Cromartie, fourth Duke of Sutherland. As a director of the Highland Railway, the Duke exercised the privilege, originally granted to his father, of operating his private locomotive on the company's rail lines. The thirty-one-ton "Dunrobin" was both a working locomotive and a source of entertainment for the Duke and his many guests. Among the reigning monarchs known to have operated the 0-4-4 side tank engine were Alphonso XIII of Spain and Edward VII, George V, and George VI of Great Britain. During the two world wars, "Dunrobin" was conscripted to serve as a hospital train and shunting engine. When British Railways were formed in 1948, the private operating rights of the Dukes of Sutherland were revoked and the "Dunrobin" was sold. After spending fifteen years on a siding in New Romney, Kent, it was brought to Canada by a British Columbia businessman in 1965. Purchased by the provincial government in 1967, the "Dunrobin" was restored and has served at Fort Steele ever since. In 1971, it once again carried British Royalty during the visit of Queen Elizabeth II, Prince Philip, and Princess Anne.

53. The Shay

The Shay, "Robert E. Swanson," was a much more familiar type of locomotive to the residents of British Columbia. Tough and powerful, Shays played a significant role in provincial logging history.

Shays were not designed for speed, but for the maneuverability and great power required when hauling logs to the sawmills over miles of rough track with difficult grades. First produced in the 1880s, Shays were widely used in the forests of British Columbia until the 1950s, when the movement of logging operations to steeper valleys resulted in the locomotives being succeeded by heavy duty trucks. The "Robert E. Swanson," built in 1934, was one of the last Shays produced by Lima Locomotive Works. During its career, this twelve-wheeled locomotive worked in logging operations at Rock Bay, Duncan, Cowichan Lake, and Englewood, and later served as a shunting engine at Vancouver Wharves in North Vancouver. At ninety tons, the oil-burning Shay is three times the size of Fort Steele's "Dunrobin." A gift of Mr. R.E. Swanson, the Shay began its new career at Fort Steele in 1971.

54. Clydesdales

To the pre-motorized generations, the large draft horse was essential for all kinds of heavy labour. On the farm, teams were used for ploughing, stumping, and hauling logs. Towards the end of the last century when agriculture was first spreading across the present-day provinces of Manitoba, Saskatchewan, and Alberta, teams of sixteen Clydesdales pulled the early combines across the flat prairie landscapes. Used in the logging operations on the heavily forested hillsides of British Columbia, such horses had the particular advantage of being able to "snake" logs between trees and out of the bush with a minimum of damage to the ground and other trees, unlike the present-day power machinery.

The Clydesdales are just one of several breeds of draft horses such as Percherons and Belgians, which were popular in North America towards the end of the last century.

Fort Steele Historic Park acquired its first Clydesdales in 1970, from Oakalla Correctional Institute near Vancouver, B.C. There they had been used in a prison rehabilitation experiment, in which it was felt that the inmates could benefit by working with the animals. Receiving loving attention, the Oakalla horses won numerous prizes in shows held at British Columbia fairs and exhibitions, especially with the six horse hitch. When it was decided to phase the horses out of the rehabilitation programme, they were transferred to Fort Steele.

Today the "Black Clydes" carry out several duties in the park. In the spring, they pull a hay wagon for visiting school children, while in the summer they pull the stage coach and the six horse hitch — the Park's show wagon. Occasionally, one is hitched to a mower for cutting grass. Teams were also used to haul the logs for the reconstruction of the North West Mounted Police buildings, just as they would have during the last century.

55. A Chronology of Important Events

Fur Trade Era

1800   David Thompson began extensive exploration on the eastern slope of the Rocky Mountains for the North West Company.

With a party of Kootenay Indians, Le Gasse and LaBlanc were sent west of the mountains by Thompson. They were the first white men to enter the Kootenays.

1807   Thompson entered East Kootenay and built Kootenae House near present-day Lake Windermere.

1808   Thompson descended the Kootenay River to Kootenay Lake.

1809   Joseph Howse of the Hudson's Bay Company entered the Kootenays through Howse Pass and explored as far south as present-day Kalispell, Montana.

1811   Thompson opened the Columbia-Athabasca route across the Rockies and descended the Columbia River to its mouth.

1821   The Hudson's Bay Company and its rival, the North West Company, united to form a fur trade monopoly.

1843   Fort Victoria was founded on Vancouver Island to replace Fort Vancouver (at present-day Vancouver, Washington) as the HBC's headquarters west of the Rockies.

1845   Father De Smet, the Jesuit missionary who organized the Oregon missions, visited East Kootenay and baptized many Indians.

1846   The Oregon Boundary Treaty was signed and the International Boundary was extended along the 49th parallel, from the Rocky Mountains to the Pacific Coast.

1849   Vancouver Island was made a Crown Colony.

1855   First deposits of gold were discovered on the Columbia River, near Fort Colville.

The Kootenay Gold Rush

1858   The gold rush on the Fraser and Thompson Rivers began and the Crown Colony of British Columbia was created with its capital at New Westminster and James Douglas as its first governor.

1863   Joe Finlay discovered gold on Finlay Creek, a tributary of the Kootenay River.

1864   The Kootenay Gold Rush began. Gold was discovered on Wild Horse Creek, a small stream which flows into the Kootenay River just south of present-day Fort Steele. The creek quickly became the centre of the Kootenay Gold Rush. The makeshift town of Fisherville was started

116

on the west bank, and by the end of the season it boasted six general stores, four saloons, a brewery, two butcher shops, a blacksmith's shop, and a large number of miners' cabins. Gold Commissioner John Carmichael Haynes was sent to East Kootenay by the colonial administration to establish law and order and to protect British sovereignty in the region. John Galbraith began a ferry service across the Kootenay River just north of the confluence of Wild Horse Creek and the Kootenay River, on the site of the future town of Fort Steele.

1865   The Kootenay Gold Rush reached its peak, but the decline of the diggings soon became apparent. At Wild Horse Creek, the Victoria Ditch was completed and supplied water to placer claims located high off the creek bed. Hydraulic mining was introduced in an attempt to recover deeply buried deposits more efficiently. Peter O'Reilly replaced Haynes as the Gold Commissioner and the Dewdney Trail, extending from Hope to Wild Horse Creek, was completed, providing a direct link with the colonial capital at New Westminster. Fisherville was demolished because it sat on some of the richest claims, and the community of Wild Horse was established further up the bank.

1866   The Kootenay Rush started to dwindle although many Chinese prospectors were attracted to the Kootenay Goldfields.

Vancouver Island and British Columbia were united as the single colony of British Columbia, with the capital established at Victoria soon afterward.

1868   A small rush began on Perry Creek, twenty-five miles north of Wild Horse Creek.

1870   The Kootenay Gold Rush was virtually at an end.

1871   British Columbia joined Confederation as a province of the Dominion of Canada.

1874   Father Fouquet and Brother Burns established the St. Eugene Mission on the St. Mary's River.

Indian Unrest and Superintendent Samuel Steele and The North West Mounted Police in East Kootenay

1883   Since the 1870s, the Kootenay Indians had become increasingly dissatisfied by the growing white population in East Kootenay. During this year, however, Chief Isadore of the Upper Kootenay band attempted to protect the hereditary rights of his people by taking matters into his own hands in announcing to the settlers that all the ranges should be free and that no man had the right to build fences. His declaration caused considerable alarm among the white residents, who feared an Indian uprising, and led directly to the Provincial Government's first real attempt to solve the conflict between the Indians and whites in East Kootenay.

1884   Upon the recommendation of Peter O'Reilly, the Provincial Indian
        Commissioner, the first Indian reservations in East Kootenay were set
        aside and totalled some forty-two thousand acres. However, Isadore
        was dissatisfied with the land which was given to his people so the
        unrest continued to simmer.

        During the same year, two miners, identified only as Hylton and
        Kemp, were found murdered and robbed near Deadman's Creek on
        the Wild Horse-Golden Trail, and Indians were suspected of the
        crime.

1885   The Canadian Pacific Railway was completed and Golden became an
        important station for East Kootenay.

        The Riel Rebellion broke out in the North West Territories and was
        quelled after much bloodshed, but the possibility of a similar uprising
        in East Kootenay should the Indian and white conflict remain
        unresolved posed a real threat to the white settlers and government
        officials alike.

1886   Chief Isadore quarreled with Col. James Baker, a new arrival in the
        district, over the ownership of Joseph's Prairie, which Baker had
        purchased and where he had established his stock-raising estate,
        "Cranbrook." Isadore insisted that it was the site of one of his
        favourite farms and that the government had no right to give it away
        in the first place.

1887   Constable Harry Anderson, the district's law enforcement officer,
        arrested an Indian named Kapula on suspicion of murdering and
        robbing Hylton and Kemp. Outraged by this action, Chief Isadore
        and twenty-five armed braves broke open the jail at Wild Horse,
        released Kapula and ordered Anderson out of the district. The
        provincial government hastily appointed a commission which met
        with Isadore. The two parties agreed that Kapula and an accomplice,
        Little Isadore, would be turned over to the proper authorities for a
        fair trial, and that Constable Anderson should be re-instated. The
        commission decided that a detachment of North West Mounted
        Police should be sent into East Kootenay to conduct a thorough
        investigation and to insure peace.

        In late July, Superintendent Samuel Steele and "D" Division arrived
        at Galbraith's Ferry where they established a post. Steele immediately
        sent for Chief Isadore and ordered him to hand over the accused. A
        trial was held and finding the evidence insufficient, Steele dismissed
        the charges against the two Indians. The dispute over the ownership
        of Joseph's Prairie was also resolved, by recognizing Baker's claim to
        the property while Isadore received another larger and more valuable
        piece of land along the Kootenay River.

1888   Having settled the problems which had brought Steele and the North
        West Mounted Police to East Kootenay, the detachment left the

118

district in August of that year. In honour of the services rendered by Steele, the name of Galbraith's Ferry was changed to Fort Steele.

A bridge was constructed across the Kootenay River, bringing Galbraith's ferry service to an end.

Fort Steele Booms

1889   William Adolph Baillie-Grohman constructed a canal at Canal Flats to connect the Columbia and Kootenay Rivers. He had hoped that the canal would create a single waterway, allowing river steamers to travel freely up and down these two rivers, but as a commercial venture the project was a failure.

1892   Large-scale hydraulic gold mining, backed by outside investment, began on Wild Horse Creek. The North Star and Sullivan group of mines, both exceedingly rich in silver and lead, were discovered and opened the era of hard rock mining.

1893   The St. Eugene Mine was discovered.

The steamboat era on the Kootenay began with the maiden voyage of the "Annerly." It was soon joined by the Ruth, Gwendoline, North Star and J.D. Farrell, running between Fort Steele and Jennings, Montana.

1894   The Kootenay River greatly flooded its banks and washed out the bridge at Fort Steele.

The Windsor Hotel (Dalgardno) was constructed. Fort Steele's first schoolhouse was built.

1895   The Fort Steele *Prospector* began publication.

1896   Work was started on the long-delayed British Columbia Southern Railway.

Fort Steele began to boom and was regarded as East Kootenay's commercial, administrative, and social centre.

1897   A telegraph line between Fort Steele and Kalispell, Montana, was completed. Fort Steele's water tower, Masonic Hall (Opera House), Government Building, and St. Anthony's Catholic Church were constructed.

The citizens of Fort Steele came to realize that the B.C. Southern Railway would bypass Fort Steele in favour of the hamlet, Cranbrook.

1898   The last spike of the B.C. Southern Railway was driven.

The Cranbrook *Herald* began publication.

The telephone reached Fort Steele and the town's second schoolhouse and Presbyterian Church were constructed.

1900   Fort Steele began to decline as people moved to the growing town of Cranbrook.

1902　Fort Steele's population, from a high point of over 4,000 in 1897/98, had dropped to only 150, while Cranbrook had grown to more than 2,000 people in the same period.

1905　The Government offices were moved to Cranbrook.

1912　The Kootenay Central Railway reached Fort Steele.

1914　The Kootenay Central Railway reached Golden, linking the CPR main line with the B.C. Southern.

1934　Perry Creek water wheel was put into operation.

1961　Fort Steele was created a Historic Park of the Province of British Columbia.

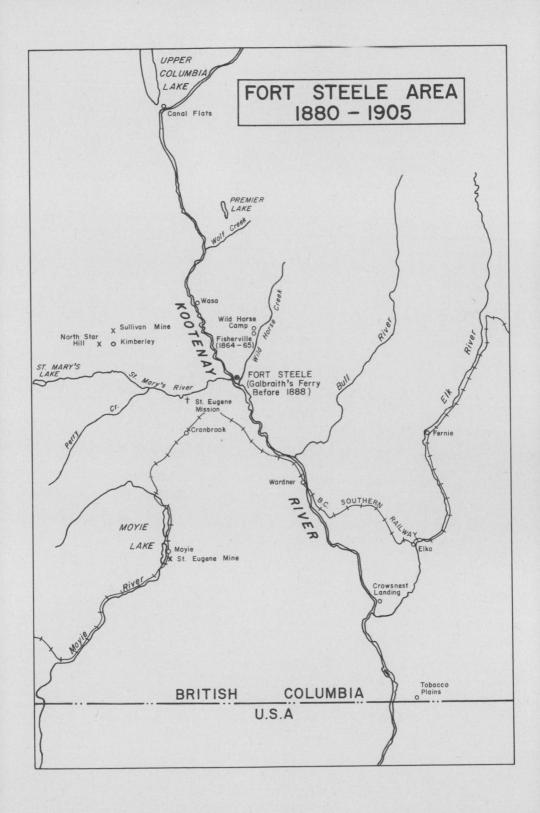

FORT STEELE AREA
1880 – 1905

UPPER COLUMBIA LAKE

Canal Flats

PREMIER LAKE

Wolf Creek

Wasa

Wild Horse Camp

Wild Horse Creek

Sullivan Mine
North Star Hill   Kimberley

Fisherville (1864 – 65)

ST. MARY'S LAKE

St. Mary's River

KOOTENAY

FORT STEELE
(Galbraith's Ferry Before 1888)

Bull River

Elk River

Fernie

Perry Cr.

† St. Eugene Mission

Cranbrook

Wardner

B.C. SOUTHERN RAILWAY

RIVER

MOYIE LAKE

Moyie
X St. Eugene Mine

Elko

Moyie River

Crowsnest Landing

BRITISH   COLUMBIA

Tobacco Plains

U.S.A

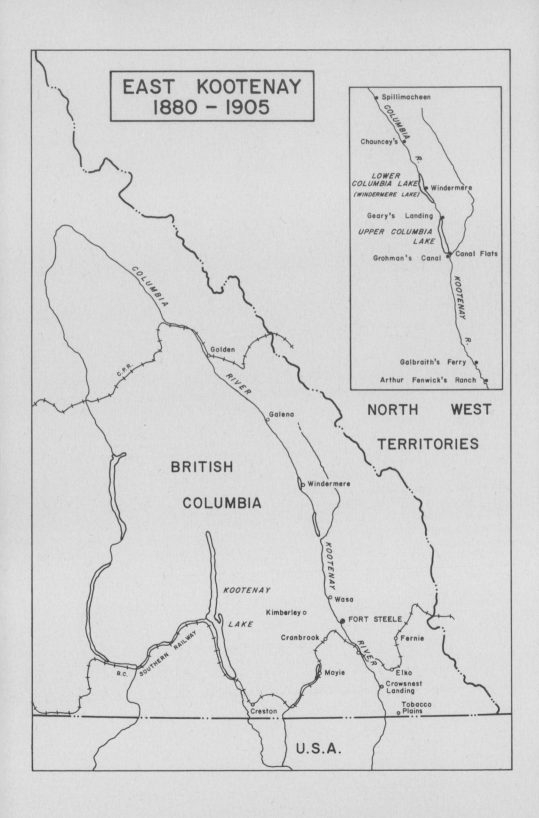

EAST KOOTENAY
1880 - 1905

COLUMBIA

Spillimacheen

Chauncey's

LOWER
COLUMBIA LAKE
(WINDERMERE LAKE)

Windermere

Geary's Landing

UPPER COLUMBIA
LAKE

Grohman's Canal

Canal Flats

KOOTENAY R.

Galbraith's Ferry

Arthur Fenwick's Ranch

NORTH   WEST

TERRITORIES

C.P.R.

Golden

RIVER

Galena

BRITISH

COLUMBIA

Windermere

KOOTENAY

KOOTENAY

LAKE

Wasa

Kimberley

FORT STEELE

Cranbrook

Fernie

RIVER

B.C. SOUTHERN RAILWAY

Moyie

Elko

Crowsnest
Landing

Creston

Tobacco
Plains

U.S.A.

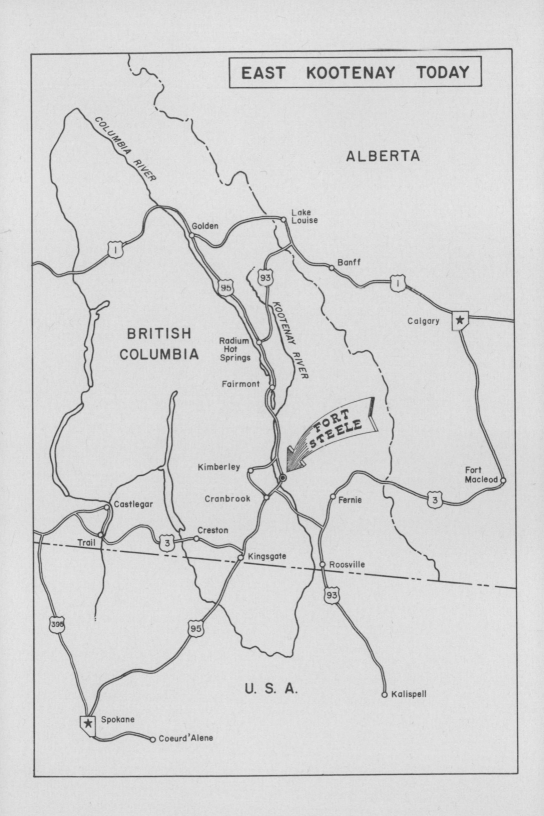

EAST KOOTENAY TODAY

Campgrounds and Points Of Interest in the Area

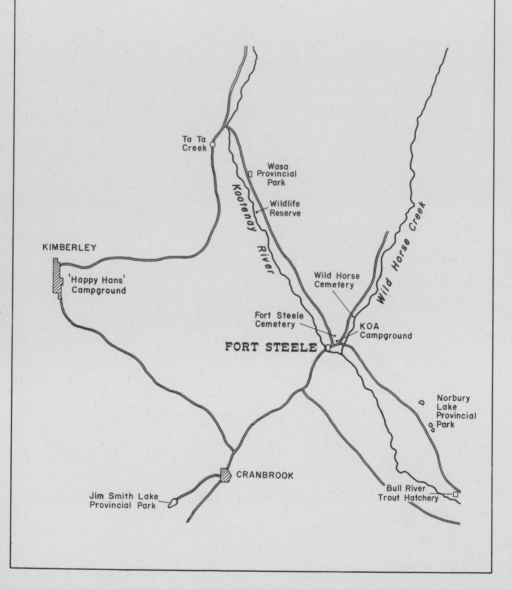

Ta Ta
Creek

Wasa
Provincial
Park

Wildlife
Reserve

Kootenay River

Wild Horse Creek

KIMBERLEY

'Happy Hans'
Campground

Wild Horse
Cemetery

Fort Steele
Cemetery

KOA
Campground

FORT STEELE

Norbury
Lake
Provincial
Park

CRANBROOK

Jim Smith Lake
Provincial Park

Bull River
Trout Hatchery